Open More Doors. Close More Sales.

The POCKET SALES MENTOR

Proven Sales Strategies at Your Fingertips

GERHARD GSCHWANDTNER
Founder and Publisher of *Selling Power*

McGRAW-HILL

NEW YORK | CHICAGO | SAN FRANCISCO | LISBON
LONDON | MADRID | MEXICO CITY | MILAN | NEW DELHI
SAN JUAN | SEOUL | SINGAPORE | SYDNEY | TORONTO

The **McGraw·Hill** Companies

1 2 3 4 5 6 7 8 9 0   DOC/DOC   0 9 8 7 6

ISBN-13: 978-0-07-147587-7
ISBN-10: 0-07-147587-7

McGraw-Hill books are available at special quantity discounts to use as premiums and sales promotions, or for use in corporate training programs. For more information, please write to the Director of Special Sales, Professional Publishing, McGraw-Hill, Two Penn Plaza, New York, NY 10121-2298. Or contact your local bookstore.

CONTENTS

CHAPTER 1

Generating Leads

PROSPECTING: DEVELOPING NEW LEADS

"Generating leads is akin to building the Alaskan pipeline," says Jamie Teschner, vice president/regional manager of American Century Investments Services Inc., a mutual fund company that sells to banks, trust companies, and brokers. "You build a client base, you integrate services, and then you'll start to see the oil flow in the form of business and new leads."

So how do you build the pipeline and get that oil flowing? Starting from scratch or making cold calls doesn't have to be as labor-intensive as the Alaskan pipeline if you know where to begin.

Janelle Patterson, a Honeywell service account specialist, spent a lot of time digging through Honeywell's archives of everyone who purchased Honeywell's products or services out of their Washington, DC, location in the last 10 to 15 years.

Patterson, who now gets most of her leads through referrals, also targets companies via the Internet. "I look at what markets we've been successful in and then research those types of companies and learn from their Web sites," she explains. "The Internet allows me to do my homework before I call.

"I also get a lot of leads from the field technicians," Patterson continues. "They can find out firsthand if the customer has a service contract. If not, it's a lead for me. I keep an open line of communication with the field technicians by giving them feedback, and that helps me to generate even more leads."

Another way Patterson gathers leads is through "competitor sightings." "If I see a competitor's van at a building, I know that prospect uses our type of services," she says. "I call and ask if I can send them my card in case they decide to switch vendors. It works; I've gained many leads this way!"

Business, social, and community relations also offer all types of leads. Get out in your community—teach a course, coach a team, sponsor a charitable event, or join a civic, non-profit, or networking group. The opportunities are endless.

Purchased lists are another good way to begin if you get a good, qualified list that targets the niche you are after. Advantages include cost and time savings, but remember that the list is also accessible to your competitors.

THE OIL FLOWS

Existing customers offer the strongest opportunities to help generate leads. Once you've established their trust, ask for referrals. "Don't overlook your relationships and the networks that form from those relationships," says Teschner. "Each of

LEAD GENERATION SKILL SET

1. **Investigate market segments:** Check out market segments where your company is successful and explore them via the Internet.

2. **Use your field team:** Sometimes your field team can give you the most reliable leads.

3. **Follow your client:** If your client leaves one company to go to another, don't be left behind. You've worked hard for that client's trust.

4. **Use prequalified lists:** Make sure you have a good list, and then keep smiling while you're dialing.

5. **Ask for referrals:** This is often your best way to generate leads.

6. **Join business/nonprofit groups:** Do your part and leads will follow.

those alliances offers a wealth of information to help your career progress."

"Generating leads from referrals gives you an advantage," says Patterson. "Referrals help you develop a rapport and increase your credibility."

Teschner also advises that you follow your customers' careers. "Just because they leave company A doesn't mean you can't call on them at company B," says Teschner. "Develop those relationships and maintain them. They are the core of your business."

How do you earn the respect and trust that will give you referrals? Having a good product and coming through for your clients are two ways. "I've always positioned myself as part of their company," says Teschner. "I go to bat for them; I'm on their side. That helps me build important relationships, which in turn gets me more leads."

IS IT OIL OR SLUDGE?

So how do you know if someone is a real prospect or just wasting your time?

"I spent a lot of time in my early sales days being a professional visitor. I spent time with people who really had no need for my products or services, but just liked talking," says Patterson. "I finally learned to be a better qualifier over the phone, to make sure the person has a compelling reason to change vendors or use my product or service."

In some businesses it's hard to qualify over the phone. In that case Teschner advises making an appointment to spend at least a half hour with someone. "After that amount of time, you'll be able to tell if someone has a real vision," says Teschner.

There are some profitable and simple ways to prospect—use your networks, do your homework, and ask for referrals. But no matter how you prospect, do it consistently.

TIPS FOR GENERATING GOLD SALES NUGGETS FROM YOUR PROSPECTING EFFORTS

If you're ever in a grocery store and you notice another shopper acting a little strange—dwelling a bit too long on certain

TIPS FOR GENERATING LEADS

1. **Discuss your solutions with existing customers:** If they understand the value you offer, ask if they know anyone else who might benefit from your products or services. Then ask your customers how you should contact the referred prospects.

2. **Before attending a trade show, find out if you can obtain a list of preregistered attendees:** Then send these individuals a mailer or e-mail introducing yourself and inviting them to visit your booth at the show.

3. **Check your orphan file:** Among your inactive accounts, eliminate all customers who, for whatever reason, will never buy from you. Call the remaining people to find out why they're not buying from you anymore and what it would take to change that.

4. **Become an expert:** Submit articles to industry journals, trade magazines, and newspapers. By providing quality, useful information to the public, you gain credibility and become the first person customers call when they need your services.

5. **Network with networkers:** Is there someone among your social or business contacts who is a great networker, a person who just seems to know everyone? Are there more than one? Put these people's strengths to work for you. Get them on the case for you, drumming up names and numbers of your likely customers.

products, turning them over in her hands, and inspecting them closely—don't be surprised. It may just be Lisa Reimer, a sales professional with Star Container, out trolling for customers.

"We manufacture plastic PET containers, the kind you might see with 2-liter bottles or other containers for the food and beverage industry," she explains. "A lot of times I get leads by going to grocery stores, club stores and canvassing them for potential products that are in the PET material or that might be right for conversion from glass to plastic. I look on the shelves, turn containers over, and see what we're dealing with."

Reimer adds that, with her notepad and pen, store clerks frequently mistake her for a mystery shopper. But she doesn't let them deter her from her goal: ferreting out new business. Following are a few additional Reimer tips to effective prospecting.

1. **Make the time:** "Prospecting is probably the least attractive part of the selling job, but it's absolutely critical, particularly when you're doing well. That's when you tend to neglect it, and then something comes up that you're not expecting. You may lose a big customer, and you're left in the lurch. In our business it can take 6 to 10 months for business to bear fruit, so you need to keep prospecting constantly."

2. **Any report in a storm:** "At Star we report to our sales manager monthly on our prospecting pipeline. It's an Excel spreadsheet with the customer's name, the product, price per thousand, start date, and how the account will affect this year's number, and we add a commentary. It may seem like a chore to do every month, but it's really helpful in keeping you fresh and constantly updated

because you know you have to turn it in. We just started it 10 months ago. Before, we just did it whenever we thought to, but now I take it out every week and work on it. It's been very helpful to me."

3. **Get fresh:** "For a variety of reasons, I like to prospect on Monday mornings. First, that's when I'm at my freshest and so are your customers. Plus, you're more likely to catch people then. Sometimes I'll even call before eight o'clock because often decision makers come in early, before the secretaries, and that's a good time to reach them. But because it requires so much energy and you need to convey a positive attitude, prospecting when you're fresh makes the best sense."

4. **Noble salvage:** "When I run into a brick wall with a certain customer, I'll ask, 'Do you know anyone else who might be interested in using our product?' It is a good way to salvage something out of a prospect who has turned out to be something of a dead end."

10 WAYS TO GENERATE LEADS THROUGH NETWORKING

Networking works, if you know the purpose behind it: to give and get useful information. Every time you encounter someone, you have the chance to do business. Go to business mixers. Join networking clubs. By sharing contacts, ideas, and leads, everyone benefits. Done properly, no one feels pressured. So says author, speaker, and trainer Arnold Sanow, who offers 10 ways to make networking work for you.

1. **Establish goals:** What kinds of people do you want to meet? How many do you want to meet? What kind of events will you attend?

2. **Be specific:** Know the type of person you want to meet. Sanow looks for people who hire trainers and speakers, including meeting planners, human resource directors, training chief, and personnel directors.

3. **Devise a 16-second sizzler:** Tell others about your work in 16 seconds or less. Otherwise, you'll lose your listener.

4. **Get out there:** Attend meetings. Get involved in civic, fraternal, church, professional, and other groups. Get involved.

5. **Raise your profile:** Never turn down the chance to speak to a group. Volunteer to be an officer in a club. Write articles for trade publications. Greater visibility increases credibility and spurs people to seek you out.

6. **Make contacts:** No matter the situation, take risks. If you want to meet someone, go ahead. The wider your circle of contacts, the more possibilities will await you.

7. **Ask and you shall receive:** You've got to ask. How else will you get what you want? When you see someone who can help you—and whom you can help—take the obvious step.

8. **Stay in touch:** Networking is one thing; follow-up is something else. Here's good advice: Keep in contact with each person in your network every couple of months, at least. Phone; suggest lunch. Send your newsletter or an article relevant to their work.

9. **Go nowhere without your tools:** Carry business cards and promotional material everywhere. Sanow recommends putting your picture on business cards.

10. **Give more, get more:** Return favors. When someone gives you anything—a referral, new business, whatever—return the favor. Pronto. Mail a handwritten thank-you note, too.

ONCE YOU HAVE A LEAD, GIVE THEM THE VIP TREATMENT

As a rule, the better your attitude, the better your sales and productivity. But while you're trying to keep your own spirits up, don't forget to give your buyers a boost. When your prospects feel good about themselves, they may be more receptive to your message and to the idea of buying. Combine these tips with some genuine sincerity to help put your prospects in a buying frame of mind.

1. **Sincere compliments may get you somewhere:** You might feel like your prospects can see through your attempts to flatter them into buying. If your compliments are insincere, they probably can. To avoid looking like a phony, don't offer a compliment you don't really mean. Flattery sounds more sincere when it's specific, so if you really love your prospect's new briefcase, include a specific reason (the color, the material, the style). If you're ready to replace your briefcase, ask your prospect where he got his. When you can, use sincere flattery to help reassure your prospects that they have good taste and are capable of making intelligent buying decisions.

2. **Make your prospect feel important:** VIPs are usually VIPs for a reason—they're powerful, intelligent, well respected, and/or high achievers. Reassure your prospects that they have these qualities and you'll help make their buying decision look easy. Start by listening carefully to them and asking for their opinions and feedback on your products or other business issues. On your first call, avoid calling your prospect by their first name. Tell them you know how busy they must be and that you don't want to take up a lot of their time.

3. **Love your prospects:** We don't always love the people who love us, but it definitely helps. Being with people who like us makes us feel likable and fun to be around, and given a choice, most of us would probably rather be popular than disliked. Find ways of telling your prospects you like them. If you're late for an appointment and they're understanding, if they listen to you carefully, if they always try to be polite, tell them how much you appreciate it. Say "I really enjoy working with people like you" or "I really value having you as a customer." When you call on the phone, let your voice reflect your enthusiasm for talking to them and tell them it's always a pleasure to speak with them.

4. **Be your prospect's reflection:** Not only should you strive to like your prospects, it helps to try to be like them as well. Sharing many of the same characteristics with your prospects gives them one more reason to trust you and believe that you understand what they need. To find out what you and your prospects have in common, be

observant. Take note of the things you see in their offices—photos on the desk or walls, awards, artwork by an artist you both may admire. During the course of polite conversation, ask if they have any special interests or hobbies or what their favorite sports teams are. When you discover a similarity between you and your prospect, refer to it regularly throughout the course of your contact. Show your prospects that you share common interests, and you might end up sharing a profitable business relationship as well.

Having the sharpest selling skills and the best-quality product might not get you the sale if your prospect isn't in the mood to buy. Buying involves risk, and many prospects won't take a chance unless you make them feel confident about themselves and their decision. To get a sale that makes you feel good about yourself, start by making your prospects feel good about themselves.

CHAPTER 2

Cold-Calling Techniques

HOW TO HANDLE COLD CALLS WITH EASE

If you hate to make cold calls, you're not alone. A majority of sales professionals rank cold calling as the most unpleasant part of their work.

Most salespeople would rather avoid cold calls than put themselves in a position of facing potential rejection. Although there's no question that unsolicited calls are usually greeted with variations of a "don't bother me" response, you can learn to handle your initial interaction with your prospective customers with power and control.

How can you make cold calls work for you? Predict that your potential customer is going to greet your call with some degree of hostility—the normal suspicion of an unsolicited intrusion. This defensive reaction has nothing to do with you. It is an automatic, built-in protective response. Therefore, you must plan that, in 30 seconds or less, you will be hit over the head with an objection to whatever you are offering.

"I'm not interested." "I'm too busy right now." "Call back in six months." "Send a brochure." The excuse given to get rid of you very often has little to do with what is really going on in your potential customer's work life. Your prospect is simply trying to defend his territory.

The objection that your prospect will give you has little to do with what she really needs. The business world is more competitive than ever. To survive no company can afford to say no to an opportunity to increase sales, reduce expenses, increase profits, increase productivity, and improve customer service. Every company must take advantage of new technology and new ways to sharpen its competitive edge and increase its market share. If a company isn't moving forward, it will be left behind.

When your prospect is putting you off, he is really saying that he's too busy putting out fires to do any strategic planning. When he says to call back in six months, he is really saying that he hopes to have more time to plan later. When he says he's not interested, he is actually saying that he is not interested in wasting his time with a salesperson who will not add to his bottom line.

Obviously, you want to tune into the underlying message. You want to hear what your prospect is thinking, and you can be sure that your prospect is thinking about these very real problems all the time.

Another thing you can be sure your prospect is thinking about is how his performance looks to his superiors. You can be certain that your prospect is always thinking about how he can stand out by coming up with an approach, a program, or a product that will truly reflect well on the positive evaluation of his performance.

Now that you can appreciate the difference between the verbal rejection and the unstated need, you are ready to handle the objections that result from a self-initiated call. You start your call by making an introductory statement about yourself and your company. Then you engage your prospect in questions designed to bring to the surface problems related to low sales, high expenses, low productivity, problems with customer servicing, and the need to increase profits and market share. You conclude with a request for a brief meeting where you can give an overview of what your company can offer in these areas.

Now, the challenge is on. Here come the predictable objections. Acknowledge the objections, without getting hung up on them, and move on quickly to the unstated need:

CUSTOMER: I'm not interested.

YOU: I wouldn't expect you to be interested in something you know so little about. But may I ask, are you interested in reducing your expenses?

CUSTOMER: I'm too busy to meet with you.

YOU: Well, time is certainly a problem for all of us. If time wasn't a problem, would you be interested in increasing the productivity of your managers/programmers/payroll department?

CUSTOMER: We don't have the budget.

YOU: Budget constraints certainly exist for most companies right now. If budget wasn't a problem, would you be interested in increasing your sales? If I could show you how this product or service could pay for itself within six months and increase your sales within your fiscal year, would you be interested in knowing more about it?

Once you establish that an interest exists in principle, you can then move to a close with: "In that case, I recommend that we meet for 20 minutes so that I can make you aware of some profitable opportunities for your company. Can I see you on Tuesday?"

This approach works. By separating the stated verbal objection from the underlying need, you will be able to take control of the predictable defensive response. Once you practice making some initial calls, your fear of rejection will become a fear of the past. With practice, you will be able to handle cold calls with ease.

SIX STEPS TO COLD CALLS THAT CLOSE EVERY TIME

Cold calling can be a hit-or-miss game. Many top salespeople spend a full day every week simply cold calling to build their prospect base. Yet other salespeople seem unable to make cold calling a regular and lucrative part of their sales strategy. With the right cold calling strategy, though, you can stack the odds of success in your favor. To keep your prospect's attention long enough to present your product, use this six-step cold-calling action plan every time you pick up the phone or walk through a prospect's door:

1. **Arouse your prospect's curiosity:** Within the first minute of your conversation, you have to give your prospect a

reason to let you continue. What can you say about your product that will make your prospect sit up and take notice? If you've done your homework, you might have an idea of how your product can help meet your prospect's most important goals or solve her most serious problems.

Make a brief, specific statement about your product's capabilities and how it will increase your buyer's business or help her do her job more effectively. Describe how your product (or a similar but inferior version) is helping your prospect's competition. Chances are, your prospect will want to know what's in it for her, so be prepared to tell her quickly and concisely.

2. **Qualify the prospect:** As you're trying to raise your prospects' interest in you, find out how interested you should be in her. Does her company have a legitimate need for your product? Can the company afford to buy it? Does she seem sincerely interested in it? Prepare a list of open-ended questions that uncover goals, needs, budget, and anything else you need to know to determine whether you and your prospect are a good business match. As always, listen more than you talk. If you can't identify a need for your product, admit it. Your prospect may reward your honesty with a good referral.

3. **Mirror your client:** As a rule, people like to buy from other people like them. To sell to a variety of clients, you have to adapt your approach and be able to communicate with each prospect at his or her individual level.

To show prospects you're "one of them," adopt some of their gestures and mannerisms. Let your tone, vocabulary, and rate of speech reflect theirs.

Your goal should be to sound more like your prospects without making it obvious to them. Watch for clues the moment your walk in the door. Did the prospect greet you with a smile? Engage you in small talk? Want to get straight down to business? Show your prospect that you're two of a kind and you'll boost your odds of making the sale.

4. **Build rapport:** Great rapport can help you get the sale as easily as a great product at a great price. Building rapport with prospects encourages them to trust you, which makes it easier for them to buy from you. Before you meet with or speak to your prospects, find out what you have in common with them.

   When you call the receptionist to schedule an appointment, do a little research on your prospect. You might ask about your prospects' hobbies, favorite sports teams, or favorite foods or if they've celebrated a recent birthday, anniversary, or other special occasion. Explain your questions by saying that you don't intend to pry or be nosy, but that you always like to find out a little about your prospects before you meet them.

5. **Act natural, but professional:** When you meet with your prospect, remember that you're not just selling your product, you're selling yourself. Make sure your hair, clothes, and posture make a positive statement about you. Project an air of quiet confidence. If you talk too

much, or act uptight or nervous, you might raise your prospects' suspicions. Rehearse your presentation for your colleagues and have them critique your performance. Guide your prospects to a buying decision without making them feel like they're being sold.

Based on the impression you make, your prospect may decide to buy from you once, over and over again, or not at all.

6. **Prepare for your next call:** Make notes on your first call to help you prepare for the second. Write down what you talked about to build rapport, your prospects' level of interest, the questions they asked, and the important points of your presentation.

   On your second appointment, be prepared to refresh your prospect's memory of the first one. Note the appearance of the office to help you decide how to set up a slide presentation or how you'd like to physically set up your next call. When you ask for your second appointment, get a specific date and time to return. Finally, be sure to ask for the sale on the first call to help make sure there will be a second.

Cold calling leaves a lot to chance, which means your sale can hinge on how well you've prepared for your calls. A good strategy gives you a chance to examine the obstacles that stand between you and a sale and to plan how you'll overcome them. It also gives you the confidence to know you can face anything your prospects throw at you. No one can guarantee cold-call success, but persistence and thorough preparation can make sure the odds are in your favor.

14 FIELD-TESTED TIPS FOR COLD CALLING ON THE PHONE

Rebecca L. Morgan, owner of Morgan Seminar Group, specializes in presenting seminars for organizations on time management, sales, and customer service. These are her winning strategies for success for cold calling over the phone.

Do you hate to make cold calls on the phone? If you do, you're not alone. The reason that most salespeople hate telephone cold calling is that they haven't defined and then refined their telephone pitch. Here are 14 easy to use telephone cold-calling tips to turn this onerous task into pleasurable profit.

1. **Only give your company name to the receptionist if it's well known:** Receptionists weed you out automatically or ask screening questions if they've never heard of your "calling for Mr. Prospect, please."

2. **When you talk to your prospect, eliminate "How are you today?"** It sounds amateurish. You are a professional, not just another salesperson. Project class from your opening through your close.

3. **Avoid "You don't know me":** Give this information in a more positive, upbeat way by saying, "We haven't met yet."

4. **Get the prospect's permission before asking questions:** Don't jump right in and do a needs assessment. Ask: "In order to see if our services may be useful to you, may I ask you a few questions?" You'll stand out as an exceptional salesperson.

5. **Ask questions:** Get the prospect involved instead of talking at him. Ideally, you will do 25 percent of the talking and the prospect will do the rest. Probe for critical information like, "Could you tell me who makes the decisions about purchasing your widget parts?" Obvious questions such as "Would you like to increase your profits?" will irritate, not stimulate the prospect.

6. **Be polite and courteous:** Use phrases like "with your permission," "may I," "thank you," and "I appreciate your time."

7. **Sound businesslike:** Be flexible and laugh if it's appropriate, but don't waste time by joking around. Match the other person's tone. Deepen your voice while keeping up your volume. Deep voices are perceived as more powerful.

8. **Be friendly and enthusiastic:** Let your natural excitement in your product come across—without sounding like a cheerleader. Put a smile in your voice.

9. **Occasionally use the prospect's name:** Calling a prospect by her name is a compliment, unless it's overdone. If you use it every third sentence, it will sound insincere.

10. **Show you're listening:** Paraphrase what the prospect tells you and ask for clarification if something is unclear. While the prospect is speaking, use "I see," "right," and other vocal cues to demonstrate that you're following along.

11. **Plan the timing of your calls:** Executives are often approachable on Mondays and Fridays, during lunch, and at the very beginning and end of the day. Often you can get through to the top person because the secretaries are out.

12. **Always leave your name:** Even though you don't expect the prospect to return your call, leave a message so that your name is familiar the next time you call.

13. **Always return phone calls:** If you can't personally return the call, ask someone else to contact the person for you. You never know who will be calling with a lead or an order.

14. **Make it a game:** For instance, some life insurance agents celebrate the no's because the statistics show that for every 24 no's, there'll be one yes. Remember that each no brings you closer to a sale.

Telephone cold calling isn't easy. But with some guidelines and a little planning, you can use it as a chance to increase your profits. Start putting your newly refined selling skills to work for you today.

APPOINTMENT-SETTING TIPS

1. **Listen carefully:** Resist the urge to cut your prospects off. Listen for their emotions and use them to plan your responses.

2. **Restate ambiguous language:** If your prospects try to brush you off or hide a need, paraphrase them more clearly, and end your statement by asking, "Am I understanding you correctly?"

3. **Don't ask whether your prospects will see you, ask when:** Offer a choice of two dates in the very near future.

CHAPTER 3

Leaving Voice Mail

GETTING PAST VOICE MAIL: HOW TO UTILIZE VOICE MAIL TO YOUR ADVANTAGE

Nobody can deny that today's advanced communication tools are a boon for salespeople. We have faxes, Web sites, e-mail, pagers, mobile phones, caller ID, and laptop computers: all allow the professional salesperson to get more done, more efficiently.

Still, some of these tools present their own specific challenges to salespeople, and voice mail is one such example. While it allows users the convenience of accessing their messages anywhere and anytime, it can hinder salespeople from actually talking to a prospect. Customers can use voice mail to hide behind, but "If you can't tell them, you can't sell them." So how do you get around voice mail or at least make it work for you?

Tony Merlo, senior sales executive for First American Real Estate Information Services, uses a number of tactics in dealing with voice mail.

"In many respects, voice mail is the bane of our industry. But it's here to stay, so we need to learn how to deal with it," says Merlo.

"I start out making the obligatory one or two calls, the first having just basic information, and I add more details with each call I make," he says. "I don't want to 'spill my candy in the lobby' by giving the prospect everything up front, and I try to incorporate more needs in each message.

"Before I make a third call, I'll send either an e-mail or snail mail to the prospect and refer to it in the call. I may also drop the name of someone they might know in the industry and try to give the prospect more detailed information. If I actually get a live person on the other end of the line, I'm off to the races. If I don't, I'll leave the exact date and time that I'm going to call him next, and I make sure that come hell or high water, I'm on the phone to him at that time.

"If I don't get through on that call, I'll leave a message saying I'm planning on being in his area on a specific date and if they have a sincere interest in my product and meeting with me to call me back," Merlo says.

"I normally have a 60 to 70 percent success rate by doing it this way," he notes. "At the very least, I'll get a secretary or assistant calling me back either to tell me the prospect isn't interested or to set up an appointment."

Winchester Printers salesperson Dave Regan advises salespeople to make sure they listen to the customer's voice message and leave messages that have value to the prospect and create a sense of urgency.

"On the first call, the salesmen should carefully listen to the voice of the prospect to get an idea of what type of person he is," says Regan. "Sometimes I don't even leave a message the first time and instead call back the next day.

"It's important that you leave a message that points out a benefit for the prospect, and be sure to entice him to want to call you back by a certain time or date," he says. "You need to sound like somebody that a prospect would like to meet, and sincerity plays a big role. You only get one chance to make a good first impression, so you have to be careful what you say and how you say it."

Regan agrees that voice mail can be effective if it's used in conjunction with letters, e-mail, or a visit and says, above all, don't get discouraged if their voice mails aren't returned.

"For some customers I've used a combination of voice mail, notes, and spontaneous visits," he says. "In one case it took me two years of calls and spontaneous visits before I actually got the opportunity to quote on a simple print job, and I got the business.

"Don't give up after the first one or two voice mails," Regan says. "You have to convince the prospect that you know what you're talking about and can help him, so say it in a way that's interesting."

"Salespeople have a love/hate relationship with voice mail, but the reality is you're either going to have to learn how to play the e-mail game," he says, "or you're just not going to get in."

VOICE MAIL SKILL SET

1. Determine exactly what you want to accomplish with your call. Define your objective and tailor your voice mail to it.

2. Make your message concise and to the point. With each message you leave, add a little more information to arouse the customer's curiosity.

3. Insert a customer benefit into the message to give them a reason to call you back.

4. Differentiate your message from the others and create a sense of urgency.

5. If you're having trouble getting through, utilize such other communication tools as faxes, e-mail, and letters, and refer to them in your voice mail.

6. Try to find another contact within the company to help you connect with your prospect.

7. Call early or late, and vary your calling times. You may get lucky and catch the customer before or after a gatekeeper is in.

8. Use humor in your voice mail to make your message stand out from the others.

9. Don't give up if your voice mails don't get returned after the first few calls. Since voice mail is here to stay, you must integrate it into your sales efforts.

TIPS TO MAXIMIZE YOUR VOICE MAIL MESSAGE

It's unlikely that your outgoing voice mail message will ever close any deals for you, but it may well scare a few off. Your primary goal with the outgoing message is to get as many of your callers as possible to leave you coherent, actionable messages. Karl Walinskas, owner of The Speaking Connection, offers the following seven tips for putting your best-recorded-voice forward:

1. **Short and snappy, please:** No one wants to listen to an elaborate story when all they want is to let you know they called. Ideally, your message will identify you, then offer callers an opportunity to press a button to skip straight to the beep. And be sure to let callers know how to get hold of you.

2. **Who are you?:** "Hello. You have reached the voice mail of the President of the United States" is a straightforward and effective opening because it identifies the person and his position. Anyone trying to reach the Supreme Court's Chief Justice will hang up. If you find you frequently receive messages for another person or department, you may want to include a line like "If you're trying to reach the Vice President, call his undisclosed location at extension 12."

3. **Keep it up:** Listening to your message should not make the caller wonder whether you just found out about negative lab results. Make sure your message is upbeat and clear—as if to communicate that the caller will be genuinely pleased once the two of you do get the chance to speak.

4. **Give 'em an out:** Regardless of the message they hear, some people simply will not "talk to a machine." For them, you may wish to include a way they can be routed to a live human—even if that's someone who will simply take a message for you.

5. **Give 'em an E:** Rather than redirecting callers to your cell phone, where they may just get another message, consider offering your e-mail address. That way they can get in touch with you, and you don't have to bother taking down yet another message from an already clogged in-box.

6. **Marching orders:** There's nothing wrong with telling people precisely what you want them to do when leaving a message. Here are a few key questions you may wish them to address:

   - Who are you?
   - What is the purpose of your call and its importance?
   - Should I return your call, and if so, when?
   - What is the best way to reach you when I do reply?

7. **Throw them a bone:** Rather than sending callers away from leaving a message disappointed that they haven't reached you, consider offering a button option that leads them to some added value. Some ideas include the following:

   - To hear today's travel forecast, press 5.
   - To hear a description of the difference between variable and fixed-rate mortgages, press the star key.
   - Want a quick laugh? Then press 8 for the joke of the day.

TO ADD URGENCY, HAVE AN ANGLE

When you leave a voice mail message for customers and prospects, try to imagine them as they listen to the message. "Hello, this is Bob from United Catheters. I'm just, um, I just wanted to talk to you about purchasing some of our, um, catheters. Call me back if you're interested." Would you return Bob's message? No way, right? Here are some guidelines to leaving a compelling message that gives your customers a little urgency:

1. **Feel their pain:** If you've already met with the prospect and identified a possible need, refer to that pain point in your message: "Ann, this is Fred from Finger Puppets R Us. I'm calling because I think I may have a solution to the problem with cuticle chafing you mentioned in our last meeting. My number again is . . ."

2. **Don't sell:** People will rarely return calls just for the opportunity to be sold. Couch your message in terms of solving problems, moving forward with an issue, answering questions, and so on.

3. **Sound important:** Mention in your message that you're calling from Corporate Headquarters, or if that's not true, from some similarly impressive-sounding edifice. You want to create the image that you work in the kind of place where people expect their calls to be returned (even if your home office is really a converted treehouse in your backyard).

4. **Add an air of mystery:** Consider leaving only your name and phone number. Some message recipients will have their interest piqued enough to call you back—just to find out who this mysterious "Alan Smithee" is.

GETTING CUSTOMERS TO CALL BACK

For salespeople, voice mail is a boon and a burden. You want to let your prospects know you called, but the time you spend leaving messages is wasted unless they call you back. Follow these tips on your next calls to help leave messages that get a response.

1. **Expect to reach voice mail:** If you make a call expecting to speak with the decision maker only to get voice mail instead, the message you leave might reflect your disappointment. To leave a compelling message, you have to anticipate getting your prospect's voice mailbox and be prepared with an attention-getting message.

2. **Tell your customers what's in it for them:** Bear in mind that your prospects probably won't be interested in buying a product, but they will be interested in solving a problem or otherwise improving their situation. Make the focus of your message a specific benefit that's meaningful to your customer: "Mr. Jones, this is Diana Smith of ABC Company. I'd like the opportunity to demonstrate how we've helped businesses like yours increase their productivity by X percent. Can we arrange to meet on Thursday afternoon? My number is 408-555-1234."

3. **Keep it short:** To learn how to condense your message into 15 to 30 seconds, pay attention to the commercials you see on TV. Television advertisers know they have a limited amount of time to grab listeners' attention and convince them to buy what they're selling, so they know what it takes to get a lot across in just a little time.

4. **Prepare your message in advance:** Instead of trying to improvise your message in the time you have before the beep, write down what you want to say ahead of time for maximum effectiveness. Post an index card with your

message close to your phone so it's readily available whenever you need it. If you read your message, you're more likely to speak in a monotone, so beware of sounding flat and emotionless when you use your "cue card."

5. **Make it unique:** If someone asked you to write down a salesperson's typical voice mail message, you could probably put together a message that sounds like 90 percent of those your prospects hear. Write down that "typical" message, study it, and think about how you can make yours different. For example, consider starting your message with an enthusiastic, "Hey, Mr. Smith, John Doe here!" instead of the sedate and boring, "Hello, Mr. Smith. This is Joe Salesperson."

CHAPTER 4

Winning Sales Letters

WRITE SALES LETTERS THAT WORK

Before You Start to Write

You've probably heard the old saying, "A picture is worth a thousand words." That may be true, but it is often impractical to send out mass mailings of expensive, glossy brochures and catalogs. If you follow some simple guidelines, you can paint a persuasive picture with words alone—and you won't need a thousand of them to do it.

Before you put a word on paper, though, take some time to think about what you want to say and how you can say it most effectively. Don't short-change this thinking process. For your letter to succeed, it must be absolutely clear, as concise as possible, and riveting to the reader's attention. No letter can do all these things unless it's properly planned.

Decide exactly what you want your letter to sell. Is it a product, a service, a catalog that may attract future sales? Should your letter close the sale or just pave the way for an interview?

Analyze your market. Who is most likely to respond to your offer? Address yourself to the interests and needs of the most likely buyers. If you're selling a playpen, write to new parents. If you're selling homes in an exclusive retirement community, write for an older, more affluent market.

Once you've selected your target audience, determine what will make your product or service attractive to prospective buyers. Then use your letter to make your product or service attractive to these prospects. Explain what makes your product absolutely necessary to their lives. Describe what makes it better than the competition. Use your letter to make your product sound unique and irresistible. But be sure not to overwrite; in most cases, you should limit yourself to two or three important points.

Your sales letter shouldn't just explain your existence; it should make a specific offer designed to galvanize the prospect into action. Decide what you want to offer, and define the terms. Are you offering a special price, free trial, or guarantee aimed at getting the reader to use your services immediately? Are you offering the reader more information, paving the way for further, more personal sales efforts such as catalog or a meeting with a sales representative?

Make clear what specific action you want the reader to take. Should he or she wait for your call, visit your store, send a reply card, complete an order form? Emphasize any deadlines and special offers to increase the reader's interest and sense of urgency.

Finally, try to determine how long your letter should be. The best sales letter is one that is just long enough to sell the product. That may mean three lines, three paragraphs, or three pages. A chatty letter without an obvious purpose wastes your money and your reader's time. Yet a high-ticket item may need a lot of information to persuade the reader to act.

When you review your decision on what to sell and how to sell it, put yourself in the reader's shoes. Be sure to use appropriate language for getting your message across. Make sure that if you were a prospective customer, the sales pitch would interest you, persuade you, and compel you to act.

Parts of Your Letter

THE SALUTATION

Make your salutation as personal as you can. If you are writing to a particular customer, your letter will be much more effective if you can address him or her by name.

It may be impractical to make each salutation different, but you can still personalize it. If you know something about your reader that qualifies him or her for your offer, you can use this knowledge in a salutation:

- Dear Golfer:
- Dear Gardening Enthusiast:
- Dear News Subscriber:

Or use a salutation that sets the reader apart and implies that the message is especially for him or her as part of a select group:

- Dear Preferred Customer:

    You are one of a select few to receive this offer.

THE HEADLINE

The headline—or introduction or opening sentence—is the most important sentence in your letter. It has to capture your readers' interest immediately, or they won't bother to go on. Get right to the point. Make your offer, or motivate your readers to keep on going so they can find out what your offer is.

Here are some types of headlines that are proven attention-getters:

- Ask an intriguing question.

- Announce something new, different, or free.

- Promise a powerful product benefit.

- Tell readers something they want to hear.

- Aim your offer at a select group, or word it as a "last chance."

- Tease or shock your readers.

- Tell readers how to save money or improve their appearance.

Your headline should whet your readers' appetites, encouraging them to continue reading. Make it count!

If you have an especially gripping headline, consider positioning it above the salutation, and give it added impact by running it in capital letters or underlying it.

PRODUCT BENEFITS

Your letter should emphasize how your product or service will benefit the reader. Tell potential customers what your product will do for them.

Describe only product benefits that are significant and relevant to your readers—ones they will understand and remember. For example, talk about low price or superiority to the competition. But don't just make vague claims; give a reason why your product is superior. Cite tests or endorsements that support your claims, or offer a free trial.

WRONG: Our cookware is absolutely the best you can buy. It will last forever.

RIGHT: Chef magazine has rated our cookware the best-possible value for the money. To assure you of what value, we offer a lifetime guarantee.

Your letter should concentrate on selling your product, not your company. In selling a service rather than a product, you may want to mention your company's size or the number of years it has been in business, if potential customers are likely to take that as an indication of reliability. But in virtually all cases, it's the product, not the history of your organization, that will move a reader to buy.

Rather than emphasizing your company, point out the unique features of your product and show how they make it worth buying. If appropriate, explain how your product works or how it can be used.

WRONG: XYZ Corp. has been manufacturing cookware for 75 years. We make our cookware with the greatest of care, using a process that is totally our own. We have grown from a small company to a giant.

RIGHT: For 75 years, we have been selling our cookware to chefs in the nation's finest restaurants. Now, you can get this same fine cookware at a special low price.

Beware of writing letters aimed at answering possible objections. Also, avoid spending too much time attacking your competition. A negative tone will turn readers off. Responding to possible problems may make readers aware of objections they hadn't thought of yet. Don't run down your competition directly or make hard-to-believe claims without offering evidence to back them up.

WRONG: XYZ Corp. makes the best cookware you can buy for the price. Spurred by our success, a lot of companies have created cheap imitations of our cookware. Some have even added Teflon coatings or ceramic handles in an attempt to "improve" on our design. But don't be fooled—our cookware is the unmatched original!

RIGHT: *Chef* magazine, testing the finest cookware available today, has rated ours the best-possible value for the money.

Your letter should emphasize "you," the reader, rather than "we," the company. Potential customers want to know what you can do for them, so try to do your selling from their point of view. "You" should be repeated often throughout your letter.

WRONG: We make the most absorbent diapers.

RIGHT: Your baby will stay dry for hours in No-Wet absorbent diapers.

YOUR OFFER

Clinch the sale at the end of your letter. Make clear what action you want readers to take, and make it easy for them to respond. Try to repeat how they will benefit by responding.

If possible, improve your offer by taking away some of the risk of replying. You can increase responses by offering

- A free trial
- A guarantee
- A promise that no salesperson will call
- Bonus merchandise
- A reduced price
- Credit-card payment or a "bill me" option

Direct readers to your reply card or order form, if one is included. Guide them through the steps of responding. Ask them to complete the reply form and mail it right away. Try to give your letter a sense of urgency; if a reader sets it aside for later, chances are it won't be answered at all.

Consider ending your letter with a postscript. (Some companies use a P.S. in every mailing because of its high readership.) The P.S. gives you an opportunity for an added sales message, one that almost everyone who opens your envelope will read.

- P.S. The P.S. is often the first thing the reader looks at, so make it a grabber.

Writing Tips

As you start your letter, keep in mind that you are talking to someone. Try to picture that person and write directly to him or her. Make your letters friendly and sincere.

Tell your readers why you are writing. Repeat your request often, and remind readers how they will benefit by responding quickly.

A low-key approach may work for current customers, but when writing to prospects, opt for forceful, persuasive copy. Subtlety probably won't generate enough interest among those who aren't familiar with what you do.

Be enthusiastic. Believe strongly in your own appeal and let your excitement show.

Make your letter easy to read, or people won't take the time to read it. Keep your paragraphs short—no more than six lines. Use short words. Avoid complicated sentence structures.

Using gimmicks in your letter can strengthen its sales appeal. (Be careful, of course, not to overdo them.) Some proven attention-getters include underlining important information; putting "handwritten" notes in the margin to emphasize points in the body of the letter; indenting important information to set if off typographically; using bullets, or dots highlighting information; adding postscripts; writing important words entirely in capital letters; and using two or three additional colors in the letter (for example, printing the body of the letter in black and the marginal note in blue).

EIGHT TIPS FOR CREATING NEWSLETTERS THAT HELP YOU SELL

Mary Pretzer, president of the marketing consulting firm Compact Training, offers these suggestions for managers who want to improve their company newsletters:

1. **Balance 75 percent how-to/industry information with 25 percent straight sales information:** Ideally,

you want to work additional selling points for your product or service into the how-to stories.

2. **If you have enough information to include, start as a quarterly and then increase to a bimonthly or monthly if possible:** After three or four issues, recipients will anticipate the newsletter's arrival, and if it does not arrive, you will leave them wondering whether you're still in business. Keep the newsletters coming.

3. **Use a tracking device:** Such devices include a coupon available only in the newsletter; a discount on phone orders when you use the newsletter; a special phone number for newsletter readers only (instead of installing a new line, just use a "rollover" number already installed in your phone system). These tracking devices help you determine whether customers are actually reading the newsletter and if the information you've included creates real buying "hooks."

4. **Put a price on the cover:** This subconsciously makes the information more valuable to the readers and lets them feel that they're getting a $5 value for free.

5. **Make it easy for readers to order by putting your phone number or contact information on every page:** It doesn't have to be in huge type; it just has to be readily accessible—especially to readers who only skim pages.

6. **Interviews add value:** Salesperson profiles tend to be a little tedious. Use interviews to ask salespeople about industry trends or how they have helped customers solve problems. This is much more valuable to a reader than yet another profile.

7. **Beware the glamour of gloss:** Expense does not necessarily translate into effectiveness with newsletters. Dynamic editorial content is the most important factor in creating a valuable and profitable publication.

8. **The more stories, the better:** Try to include about three or four per page. Be aware that jumping stories irritates some readers. Once you get going, try continuing stories from one issue to the next, but make sure they are stories of sufficient interest that readers will look forward to the next issue.

HARNESS THE POWER OF THE WRITTEN WORD

Considering using direct mail to generate some hot leads and fill your pipeline? Here are some suggestions for writing a sales letter that keeps the telephone ringing.

1. **Humanize your letter:** Write so it sounds like you are having a one-on-one conversation with the prospect.

2. **Use a personalized salutation:** With all the sophisticated software on the market, there is no reason why you can't address a letter to an actual person, not a position. It may cost you a few pennies more per letter, but it is worth it.

3. **Keep in mind the "Attention, Interest, Desire, and Action" formula in writing your letter:**
   - **Attention:** Use a strong opening statement or headline to capture readers' attention. Develop a hook that grabs readers and prompts them to continue to read.

- **Interest:** Expand on the benefits promised in the headline. Let prospective customers know why buying from you is in their best interest. Include testimonials from satisfied customers.

- **Desire:** Appeal to readers' emotions and their favorite radio station, "WIIFM"—What's In It For Me? Keep in mind that desire is an emotion.

- **Action:** Create a sense or urgency in your letter and ask for action. Tell readers what is expected of them. For example, you can ask prospects to fax the letter back to you with a time and a date that is convenient for you to call. If you're presenting a special offer, set a time limit for response. The idea is to say, "Do it NOW."

4. **Include a P.S.:** People often read the end of a letter first (to see who sent it), so a P.S. can help catch their attention.

CHAPTER 5

Effective E-mail

CLEAR E-MAILS ARE THE KEY TO SUCCESS

The thing about e-mails is that they're supposed to be quickly written and quickly read—the electronic equivalent of a note, not a letter. So why do we find them so hard to write? The tips in this chapter will help you keep in clear communication with your office when you're on the road.

Summarize your key point in the subject line. Instead of making your subject something generic like "Hi from Boston" or "A request," title it "Expense report deadlines."

Newspaper articles are written on the assumption that the reader may not finish the whole article. Ergo, the most important information is given in the first paragraph or "lead." Likewise, your e-mails should pack the important information in early. Instead of friendly chatting, get directly to the point and state your business in the first line of the e-mail.

If the e-mail is to make a request, follow the request with any details that the reader needs in order to do what you've asked. Also provide a specific, reasonable deadline.

E-mails tend to be informal, but that's no excuse for leaving out capitals or punctuation. This is still a professional communication, and in order to have your request taken seriously, it needs to be stated in a clear and businesslike manner.

Don't put too much information in a single e-mail. If you have several topics to discuss, it may be better to send several different e-mails, each focused on one topic. Tailor your e-mails directly to the reader. If you need one thing from the accounting department and another from purchasing, don't send both requests in a single group e-mail. The more information people have to wade through, the less likely they are to remember and promptly respond to the request you're making of them. Draft different e-mails for different needs.

HOW TO CREATE GREAT SUBJECT LINES

1. **Avoid the cliché:** Like most everyone else, your customers are wary of e-mails with subject lines containing words like "Free" or "Great Deal." Likewise, avoid multiple exclamation points.

2. **Use a benefit statement:** One good strategy is to offer a concise but specific benefit that the e-mail promises to expand upon. An example might be, "Online Auctions: A simple way to eliminate excess inventory." This

subject line should grab the attention of customers who face inventory problems and at least persuade them to read the e-mail.

3. **Play the name game:** Using a customer's name is a proven sales technique, and that's true in subject lines, too. If you know the customer's first name, consider putting it at the beginning of the subject line: "Sarah, here's some great info on effective trade show selling."

4. **Shorter is better:** If you can craft a powerful, compelling subject line in 10 words or fewer, great. Five words? Even better.

5. **Style counts:** If possible, develop a unique style that your customers and prospects can quickly identify from your subject lines. It might be that you always use high-impact questions, or maybe you throw a little humor in there somewhere. But anything you can do (in a positive way) to distinguish yourself from the parade of spam will do wonders toward getting your e-mails read.

TIPS FOR EFFECTIVE E-MAIL

With today's e-mail glut, it's more difficult than ever to persuade prospects and customers to open your e-mails. Use the following ideas to get those messages opened, read, and acted upon.

1. **Make your subject line sing:** Can you boil down your message into just a few words that will compel the recipient to open your e-mail? Think: If I were receiving this message, would I bother to open it?

2. **Get to the point:** You should begin your message with the most important information. Beating around the bush or launching into a detailed anecdote is like coming out and begging the recipient to hit the Delete key.

3. **Stay on-topic:** What is the primary message you want to communicate? Figure that out and then stick to it. Don't stray or you'll water down the impact of your e-mail.

4. **Offer direction:** Give recipients a specific action to take. Don't just suggest they visit your Web page—ask them to sign up for a newsletter, register to win something, e-mail you back—anything that will move you in the direction of a sale.

USING E-MAIL TO YOUR ADVANTAGE

In the age of overflowing e-mail in-boxes, you may be tempted to abandon the idea of trying to e-mail customers at all in favor of giving smoke signals another try. But even in the era of online clutter, there are ways to use e-mail as an effective communications tool with customers. Here are some tips:

1. **Conjunction function:** Use e-mail as just one facet of your targeted approach. You might call prospects to alert them to upcoming e-mails, then in the e-mails tell them to expect a mailer, and so forth.

2. **Key on special dates:** Whether it's about the end of the quarter, an upcoming holiday, or some industry-specific event, make your e-mail topical and time-sensitive to upcoming dates.

3. **Ask for info:** Rather than constantly trying to sell something with each message, try asking customers for more information about them that will help you with market research or product development.

4. **Personalize it:** Avoid sending mass messages out to all your customers. The goal is to make customers feel special—you don't want them to come to view you as yet another spammer.

5. **Make the subject line topic A:** Your compelling subject line is the number one key to getting your e-mails read. Spend extra time finding the perfect wording that will intrigue your customers so much they can't *not* open your message.

TIPS FOR USING E-MAIL TO E-SELL

Remember when you first got e-mail, how cool it was to check your in-box and find a new message there? How times change. Now we operate on e-mail overload, where just taking a trip to the watercooler means risking returning to face two dozen new messages. Though its luster may have worn off, e-mail remains a powerful sales tool. In *High Performance Selling: Advice, Tactics & Tools—The Complete Guide To Sales Success*, Terry Beck suggests four strategies for making sure your prospects read—and respond to—your electronic messages.

1. **Subject sizzle:** The subject line is the first thing your message recipient will see, so make it compelling. If you sell candles, don't write "Candles for sale" in the subject line. Try something with a little more jazz, like

"Brighten your day" or "Lightin' up." The key is to compose something concise that will compel people to open the message instead of hitting the Delete key.

2. **Shorter is sweeter:** No one has time to sift through lots of long e-mails. They don't want to see a parade of text staring back at them. Instead, focus on making your messages concise and to the point. This is a great way to learn how to edit yourself so that you're communicating only the essence of what you need to say.

3. **But enough about me:** Much as you think the customers want to know all about you, your company, your family, and so on, they are actually much more concerned about themselves. Imagine! So when you get to the point of the e-mail, make sure it has to do with the customer's needs and the customer's business.

4. **Where do you want me to go today?** Open your messages with a purpose and conclude with a "next step" for the recipient to take. The former will pique the recipient's interest and keep them reading, while the latter will explain precisely what they need to do to take advantage of all the wonders your company has to offer.

WHEN TO USE E-MAIL—AND WHEN NOT TO

Like the hammer and saw, e-mail and the telephone are both extremely effective tools, but only when applied to appropriate tasks. Consider the following when deciding whether to contact your customers electronically or over the phone.

1. **Are you avoiding this customer?** If you're simply trying to put off a live conversation out of fear or apprehension, then a phone call is in order. The less you want to call a customer, the more you likely should do just that.

2. **How does this customer prefer to contact you?** Some customers are more comfortable with an e-mail relationship and only require phone calls for particularly pressing matters. If a customer tends to respond to your phone calls with e-mail or to your e-mails with phone calls, that's a good indication of his or her preference.

3. **How pressing is your need?** People respond more slowly to e-mail than to phone calls, so if you want to communicate urgency, e-mail may not suffice.

4. **Will it be easier by e-mail?** Sometimes people are more willing to open up via the more indirect medium of e-mail than on the telephone. If you have incisive, thought-provoking, or possibly even personal questions you need to ask, e-mail may make it more comfortable for the customer to respond with honest answers.

5. **Do you need a permanent record?** Some customers tend to conveniently forget verbal agreements, so when dealing with such individuals, e-mail provides an electronic paper trail you can refer to for verification.

6. **Where do your strengths lie?** Do you compose compelling, well-written e-mails, or are you more effective at making your points over the phone? Whichever it is, play to those strengths whenever possible. But don't use one or the other as a crutch—evaluate every situation on

its own merits so that you use e-mail and the telephone as complementary selling tools.

E-MAILING SKILL SET

1. Be professional and courteous in your e-mail messages. Use Mr. or Ms. in the greeting.

2. Make sure that there are no spelling errors. Use spell check every time.

3. Focus on the customers' needs and send them valuable (to them) information about special promotions that they can read at their convenience.

4. Use e-mail as a convenient time-saving means of exchanging ideas.

5. Don't send too much information. Use templates and general e-mail to provide quick answers to routine questions and save your valuable time.

6. Be more sensitive and tactful than you would be in telephone or face-to-face contact. Remember that customers who read your e-mail can't see or hear you. For that reason, they will assume that you mean exactly what you say in your e-mail message.

7. Use e-mail as a supplement to telephone and face-to-face contact to build rapport with potential customers, exchange necessary information quickly, and provide superior personalized customer service after closing a sale.

CHAPTER 6

Successful Proposals

WRITING PROPOSALS YOUR CUSTOMERS CAN'T REFUSE

When a sale is just inches away from a signature on the contract and the prospect says, "Give it to me in writing," don't panic. Even if you lack confidence in the writing that's an important part of the sales process, you can learn the basic keys to writing a professional, get-the-order proposal. There are seven basic parts or section headings; these guidelines will help you incorporate them into an appealing proposal that generates sales and profits.

Defined as a specific plan of action based on a presentation's facts, assumptions, and supporting documentation, the effective proposal may increase your closing ratio, decrease selling cycle length, and set you apart professionally. It represents your recommendation as to the next steps your prospect should take to get the most from the product or service you sell.

Winning Proposal Formula

Creating consistently solid proposals requires the careful use of a proposal-writing formula or checklist. The list of seven proposal parts shown in the sidebar "Compose and Propose" helps ensure that your proposals are complete and address all of your prospect's concerns or questions. When you prepare your next proposal, use the list to make sure you've covered all the bases and that the proposal clearly states your plans for the prospect's account, cost estimates, and how the prospect will benefit by buying from you. Write concisely and try to limit the paper to a single page.

To increase your closing ratio, bear in mind that your proposal—not your product or service—often determines whether you get an order. A carefully devised plan of action designed to achieve the prospect's specific goals helps to increase customer confidence in your ability and willingness to satisfy their needs. Quality proposals reassure customers that you know where you're going, and how and when you'll get there.

COMPOSE AND PROPOSE: THE SEVEN ESSENTIAL PARTS OF A PROPOSAL

1. **Budget and overview:** This first proposal section should let prospects know up front how much it will cost to follow your recommendations. Consider the prospect's finances and remember that it's your job to offer prospects exactly what they need—no more or

less. This section should also feature a general mission statement tailored to the prospect.

2. **Objective:** The objective section should clearly define the goal your proposal is designed to achieve. You might wish to offer one tangible and one intangible objective— for instance, Cut production cost and increase customer's business by 10 percent. Help customer gain competitive advantage with greater product reliability at competitive price.

3. **Strategy:** How do you plan to meet your objective? Take two or three lines to give the prospect a rough sketch of your plans. Without going into painstaking detail, reveal the means by which you'll fulfill your proposal's obligations.

4. **Tactics:** Whereas the strategy section discussed what you're going to do, the tactics section should describe how you're going to do it. Outline the specific actions that will accomplish the objective. Walk your prospect step-by-step from the proposal to its fulfillment, and show how you intend to tailor your product or service to the prospect's unique needs.

5. **Schedule:** Your recommendation should lay out a schedule for action. Establish a time frame for decisions leading to your objective. Specific contact or shipping dates allow prospects to collect their thoughts and questions before you call, and to plan their own business agendas.

6. **Results:** Show your prospects how your action plan translates into personal benefits for them. How will meeting

> your objectives have a positive impact on the prospect's business? Make sure your results section shows your prospects exactly what they'll get for their money.
>
> 7. **Rationale:** The rationale section should present "closing arguments" that use both logic and emotion to convince prospects to buy. Use benefits—not features—to summarize why the prospect should buy now.

PUT THE "PRO" IN PROPOSAL

Whether you're a sales rep making a presentation or a young man bent on marriage, you won't get anywhere without a winning proposal. Suitors know they need to have a diamond ring, a throw pillow, and an earnest look handy, but what are the characteristics that make for an effective sales proposal? In *The Ultimate Selling Guide* sales consultant Lloyd Allard offers five key suggestions for proposals that persuade customers to say "I do."

1. **R-E-S-P-E-C-T:** How you feel about your proposal will directly affect the customer's opinion. Treat your proposal as the physical embodiment of your product or service. Hold it over your head, pass it around the room so that customers can "see" your product or service while looking at the proposal. By respecting the proposal itself, you communicate the value of your solution.

2. **Slow and steady:** Delivering a proposal is like baking a cake. Rush it and it's ruined, but take too long and it's no

better. You must ride that fine line by spending enough time to communicate your proposal effectively, but not taking so long that you bore anyone.

3. **Be a confidence man (or woman):** Deliver every point of your proposal with the conviction that the customer will agree and approve. Now is no time for humility. If you lack confidence in any part of the proposed solution, customers will pick up on your doubts and start questioning themselves.

4. **Fill needs, not wants:** Don't try to accommodate customers' every whim. Ultimately, customers look to you as the professional salesperson to design a solution that is best. You are the expert, and customers will appreciate that you have the integrity to do right by them, not just give them everything they ask for.

5. **Practice, practice, practice:** Like it or not, a sales presentation is a performance, and the more you rehearse, the better your performance will be. Practice delivering your proposal in the mirror and for friends, relatives, and anyone who will sit still long enough to watch. Not only will you be better prepared once the stage lights come on, but you'll also reinforce your own confidence in the value of your solution.

STRATEGIES FOR EVERY STAGE OF THE PROPOSAL PROCESS

"Many salespeople rely on a support staff to write proposals for them, but there are dangers in this practice," says Larry

Newman, author of *Proposal Guide for Business Development Professionals* and vice president of Shipley Associates. "Because support people can't always be with the salesperson throughout the sales cycle, often the proposal comes out with a different message than the salesperson has been sharing with the client."

That's why Newman says that it's important for sales-people to be involved with the proposal every step of the way. "Salespeople must put the strategy in writing and share it with anyone working on the proposal," he says. "If they can't, there's a problem."

Newman shares the following expertise on both proposal planning and writing.

The Planning Phase

1. **Decide who should be involved:** Determine who will be part of the proposal planning and writing process. Designate a proposal manager to manage people's roles and the overall finished product.

2. **Follow a schedule:** Develop milestones to keep the proposal on track. Allocate about 10 percent to 15 percent of your time for planning, 60 percent for writing, and about 15 percent for review.

3. **Define a baseline solution:** Outline what you are going to be proposing in high-level terms.

4. **Price to win:** Everyone has a budget; make sure you know your client's. Establish the target and determine what you can give your client for that amount.

5. **Extend the sales strategy to the proposal strategy:** The proposal must align with the same message used throughout the sales process. Collect things from the sales cycle—site visits, specific meetings—to use as examples in the proposal. The bottom line: Make things consistent.

6. **Break down the proposal to be both compliant and responsive:** To be compliant, make sure you've answered all the client's questions. Responsiveness is determined by how you solve the customer's problems. To do both, prepare an outline, identify every requirement, and allocate it to a spot in the outline.

7. **Figure out the style:** What type of format will you use? What are the standards?

The Writing Phase

1. **Prepare the first draft:** Here are some things to watch for at this stage. If several people contribute without any direction, you might have what Newman calls orphans or holes—the questions that no one bothered to answer because they didn't think it applied to them. This might mean you could be adding freebies at the end—things you didn't price out. Another problem is that multiple people might answer the same question, which could result in confusion for the customer.

2. **Don't use jargon or filler words:** Eliminate phrases like "world-class organization" and "leading-edge technology."

3. **Answer the main question in the first sentence or two:**
   Write an introduction that previews your elaboration.
   Support your answer. Readers quit reading when they
   find the answer, which ultimately means they come to a
   decision sooner rather than later.

4. **Graphic or photo captions should explain what each
   graphic means:** If you can't explain it, take it out.

CHAPTER 7

Making the Most of Trade Shows

ESSENTIAL STRATEGIES FOR BOOSTING TRADE SHOW LEADS

When prospects came to your booth at the last trade show you worked, what did you do? Knowing you only had seconds to pique their interest, did you barrage them with the features and benefits of your product or service? Or did you attempt to qualify opportunities too early? If you're like the majority of salespeople, you did some of both. Classically those are the two mistakes salespeople make in handling prospects who stop by their booth. Next time, suggests Thomas Freese, author of *It Only Takes 1% to Have a Competitive Edge in Sales* try focusing on your prospects' problems instead.

"The best way to maximize your opportunity at industry trade shows is to bond with potential buyers by talking about their problems, not your solutions," says Freese. In other words, don't bombard booth visitors with facts and statistics about your great product; instead, address the problem the product solves. Here's how: when a prospect comes into your booth and asks what you do, Freese suggests such replies as, "You know all the paperwork headaches customers are now having to put up with as a result of the new federal legislation? Our product solves this problem, and it has several other features that can make your life easier and your business more efficient."

If this sounds like an issue that's pertinent to the prospect, he'll likely ask more questions and give you the opportunity for a more in-depth conversation. If not, you'd probably have had to disqualify him later anyway.

The bottom line is if you can talk about the problems your products and services solve, you'll accomplish the dual mission of piquing the interest of passersby and weeding out unqualified leads. And as those prospects ask more questions about how your product will meet their specific needs, the opportunity for follow-up conversations and meetings increases.

One note of caution, says Freese: Resist the urge to answer every question and tell prospects everything from the booth. Doing so, he says, "would only satisfy their curiosity and eliminate the need to meet with you after the show."

HOW TO TURN YOUR NEXT TRADE SHOW APPEARANCE INTO A PROMOTIONAL EXTRAVAGANZA

Exhibiting at a trade show can either be a bountiful source of promising leads or a massive waste of time and money. It all

QUICK TRADE SHOW TIPS

Here are some quick tips for making the most of your next trade show.

1. **Ask open-ended questions, or merely introduce yourself:** Instead of asking prospects closed-end questions like "May I help you?" try, "So what brings you to the show?"

2. **Ask prospects how they would like to be contacted:** This helps avoid the frequent problem of prospects taking literature and leaving without giving you a business card.

3. **Hone your efforts so you focus on just two or three goals for the show:** Then make sure to hit all the key points with every contact.

4. **Use balloons:** Studies show that, for whatever reason, balloons attract people to trade show booths.

5. **Stand next to or in front of your display:** Avoid putting a table (or anything else) between you and your potential customers.

6. **Take advantage of the opportunity to scope out the competition:** Do a little detective work on ways you can differentiate yourself and impress clients who can't decide whether to choose you or one of your competitors.

depends on the execution. To make the most of your upcoming trade show appearance, consider the following tips from Marc Goldberg, founder and partner of the Massachusetts-based consulting firm Marketech, Inc.

1. **The right show:** Meet with every interested member of your team and determine the best shows for your company to attend. Ask yourselves the following questions:
   - Why are you exhibiting?
     - Is it to increase your name recognition and product awareness?
     - To generate leads?
     - To promote a new product you're introducing?
   - What audience do you plan to target at a trade show?
   - How do you plan to make your presentation memorable to this audience?
   - What metrics will you use to judge the show's success? Leads generated? Sales?

2. **Begin with the end in mind:** Once the show is over, you will be under a mountain of business cards and leads. Beforehand, prepare information packets to send to interested parties so that you won't be scrambling to fulfill requests as soon as you return. Plan to send the packets out more than a week after the show concludes to give your prospects time to dig themselves out as well.

3. **Pitch BDA—before, during, and after the show:** Trade show attendees arrive knowing which exhibitors they plan to seek out. Send postcards to future attendees ahead of time with a taste of why they'll benefit from dropping by your display. Also, weigh the benefits of sponsoring a hospitality suite, which can more than make up for its cost in one-on-one contact with potential customers.

GETTING THE MOST FROM EVERY TRADE SHOW

You've got a lot riding on your trade show appearance, so it's important that you make the most of it. Plan your appearance around these tips to raise interest in your booth and your product, enlarge your customer base, and make your trade show trip pay for itself.

1. **Choose a show that suits your needs:** Know what you want to accomplish at the show and how the particulars of each show can help. If more customers is your primary goal, make sure the show you choose will attract the kind of qualified prospects you need. Find out if the show features any forums, roundtables, or other events in which you can participate to learn more or position yourself as an industry expert.

2. **Schedule business meetings:** Some companies plan extensive business meetings with partners, customers, or other business contacts around show dates to maximize travel budgets and use time wisely. Make a list of the people you'd most like to see, and call them well in advance of the trade show date to arrange a meeting before their schedule is full.

3. **Make a timeline:** Create a schedule of due dates for the tasks to be completed, events to attend, and bills to be paid before the show. A successful exhibit is a lengthy series of event planning, execution, and follow-up activities that peak at the show. Keeping careful track of what you need to do helps ensure a profitable and hassle-free trip.

4. **Pick a freebie:** A useful or interesting giveaway item can help attract customers to your booth. Put some thought

into the item you choose—a memo pad with your company's name prominently featured, for example, could help remind prospects on a daily basis that you're there when they need you. Whatever you choose to give away, make sure you get visitors' names and contact information in return.

5. **Practice your opening lines and questions:** You needn't spend 10 minutes engaging the customer in idle chitchat before you get to the point and start qualifying. Brainstorm in advance and write down opening lines you feel comfortable saying, along with the questions that will tell you what you need to know about your customers. Match your opening lines and questions to your visitor's personality—more gregarious, aggressive visitors can handle more direct, open-ended questions. With more reserved, reluctant visitors, stick with easier, yes/no questions.

6. **Choose staff carefully:** The best salespeople are not necessarily the best trade show staffers. Your exhibit staff will be the only impression that many visitors will have of your company. Make sure your people are well trained to meet the public, and stress the importance of maintaining an enthusiastic and cheerful attitude even after hours on their feet.

PROFIT-BOOSTING IDEAS TO HELP TRADE-SHOW SHY SALESPEOPLE

The following strategies come from Mim Goldberg, vice president of Training at Marketech Inc.

Enthusiastic salespeople make a profitable trade show experience. To build excitement for the next show, coach your team through four common trade show fears with these strategies and turn trade show phobes into trade show fans.

1. **Change:** Help your team prepare for changes in their routines. Time may be shorter at a show, so salespeople must streamline their speech. Provide opening lines and probing questions that stimulate customer conversation. Remind them to look approachable with "open" body language and a friendly expression. Role-playing sessions let salespeople perfect their new selling style before the show.

2. **Hard work:** Your team may need time to get used to so many prospects. Encourage salespeople to schedule follow-up meetings with visitors so they can avoid giving full presentations to each one. Remind salespeople to qualify visitors before spending too much time on them. Have salespeople eat and sleep well to maintain energy.

3. **Talking to strangers:** Remind your team that booth visitors are probably already interested in your product. Suggest "Tell me" as a great opening phrase to put buyers in the spotlight. Test your team's product knowledge and offer sample responses to customer comments. Have salespeople greet buyers with a smile, a handshake, and eye contact.

4. **Giving up sales time:** With greater involvement in each phase of preparation and in the trade show itself, salespeople can understand the opportunities it presents. Meet with booth staffers to share trade show objectives and strategies. Distribute a preshow plan to build anticipation.

CHAPTER 8

Surveys That Get Results

INCREASE YOUR SALES WITH CUSTOMER SATISFACTION SURVEYS

To convince prospects that your company, product, and service are the best available, start with a customer satisfaction survey. A survey of satisfied customers gives credibility to your claims while providing the prospect with a list of referrals.

The three-step method below will satisfy your prospect's objections and set you apart from the competition.

Step 1: Develop Your Own Customized Survey

Your customer satisfaction survey should include questions that address how the customer feels about your product, your service, and, most important, you. The sample on the next page will give you a good example of how the survey should look. Make your survey easy to fill out.

For example:

- Make your survey only one page long.

- Fill out the customer's name and address.

- Use multiple-choice questions and just a few fill-in-the-blanks.

- Include a self-addressed, stamped envelope.

- Ask questions that determine how you approached, maintained, and followed up with the account before, during, and after the sale. You want the customer to see you as the main problem solver and consultant.

Step 2: Position The Survey

The following selling scenario will show you how to use your customized survey:

CUSTOMER: How do I know that your service is as good as you say it is? How can I be sure you will follow up after the sale? Every salesperson promises me the same thing!

SALES REP: I can understand how you feel. Most of my present customers say the same thing, and then I show them this. (Hand the prospect a blank customer satisfaction survey.)

CUSTOMER: A survey? So what's this going to prove?

SALES REP: (Hand the customer a self-addressed, stamped envelope.) If you'll notice, Mr. Prospect, the envelope is addressed to the president of my company. Every 30 days, each of my customers receives this survey. Our company uses these surveys to measure how the sales force handles accounts. If the president receives any bad feedback from one of my accounts, I have to answer to her personally. By giving you this survey now, my evaluation starts today, and I'm going to do everything possible to make sure that you're happy with our company, product, service, and most of all, me.

Step 3: Compile A Customer Case History

Now that you've presented the survey to the prospect, what comes next? Hard work! Collect as many completed surveys as possible. If you've been following up with your present accounts, and they're satisfied, there should be no reason why they wouldn't be happy to fill out a survey. Once you've collected the surveys, you can put together a presentation book to build a customer case history. You can even include the few bad surveys you may get, as long as you solve the problem and get an updated survey to reflect your effort. Telling a potential customer that nobody's perfect and every sales rep has a few unhappy customers is one thing, but showing the prospect how you turned those unhappy customers into satisfied customers in 30 days is what will make the difference. Going back to the selling scenario, you can see how the sales rep presents the customer case history.

SALES REP: By the way, Mr. Prospect (pull out your customer case history book), here are over 50 surveys that my customers mailed in. (Take the prospect through the surveys, highlighting important comments or ratings.) Here's a survey from one customer who had some problems with the product. And here's his next survey after I mediated between our service department and the customer and resolved the problem.

CUSTOMER: This looks impressive!

SALES REP: Then why don't we get started on making you a satisfied customer, so you can become part of my customer case history?

A customer case history book with customer satisfaction surveys is priceless. Not only will you build credibility and increase your sales, but you will have something much more valuable—a lifetime selling tool that exemplifies a proven track record.

TIPS FOR FINDING OUT JUST WHAT YOUR CUSTOMERS ARE THINKING

Salespeople love receiving customer feedback—especially when the news is good. But are you doing enough to encourage your customers to share their true feelings about your company, your product, and the service you're delivering? In *180 Ways To Walk The Customer Service Talk*, Eric Harvey suggests nine tips for filling your corporate trough with customer feedback:

1. **Dedicate a line:** Establish a voice mail or e-mail account as a direct pipeline to the owner, president, or a senior-level manager, then encourage your customers to use it. They will appreciate the access to upper-level management, and you will receive invaluable information on improving your processes.

2. **Get on board:** Put together a customer advisory board of your key clients. Bounce new products and service ideas off the board, and ask them for suggestions on improvement. Make board memberships last one year, and convene the group quarterly at a classy local restaurant.

3. *Use space wisely:* Add a brief three- to four-question customer service survey to the back of your remittance envelopes.

4. **Question everything:** Develop a customer satisfaction survey that is simple and that you can use to solicit quarterly feedback from repeat customers. Ask what they would change, add, or eliminate from your products and services.

5. **Just one more thing:** When you finish up service encounters, get used to asking customers, "What's one thing we can do to service you better the next time you call on us?" Post the responses on index cards for everyone to see, and use them as talking points for staff meetings.

6. **Prep on it:** Before asking customers "Was everything alright?" or "Did you enjoy . . .," know how you're going to respond to a no.

7. **Three strikes, you're in:** Here are the three golden customer-satisfaction survey questions:
   a. What are we doing well that we should keep doing?
   b. What are we not doing well that we should stop doing?
   c. What should we start doing that we aren't doing now?

8. **Appreciation is enough:** Whenever your customers take five minutes out of their busy schedules to do you a

favor, like answering a survey, reward them with a gift, trinket, coupon, or some other tangible token of your thanks.

9. **Duly noted:** When you follow a customer's feedback suggestion for change, let them know about it with a note and encourage them to experience the change firsthand— with more business.

CHAPTER 9

Qualifying Leads

DEVELOPING NEW LEADS INTO QUALIFIED PROSPECTS WHO HAVE THE AUTHORITY TO BUY

An essential part of any lead management program must be the phase when you determine if the lead you have is in fact a prospect.

A prospect satisfies three key criteria: (1) the prospect has a need that involves your product (2) the prospect has a budget to buy, and (3) the prospect has the authority to sign an order.

Keeping these criteria in mind, the best way to convert leads into qualified prospects involves turning lead generating and qualifying into one smoothly operating system.

Jon Spokes, advertising manager for *The Washington Times* magazine division, has trained and supervised sales reps for companies selling a variety of products and services. Spokes points out that many sales reps confuse "suspects" with "prospects." A suspect is anyone who needs or uses the type of product or service you sell. A prospect is someone who needs what you sell when you are selling it. Once you have a prospect, your lead system should kick into gear.

A good, qualified lead could be anyone who's unhappy with what he or she presently uses. In order to determine who that might be, do some legwork before you show up and start selling.

Spokes suggests, "Talk first to actual users of the product, such as clerical staff or other office personnel. For this purpose, your best contact is probably the office manager."

How do you find the office manager and get that person to talk with you? Ask whomever you can reach by phone or e-mail for the name of the office manager. You can say you'd like to send some information directly to the right person. Then you can legitimately ask for that person's name. And don't forget to get the spelling right. Once you have the office manager's name, contact that person and invite him or her to coffee or lunch. Explain that you are new (to either your job or the area), and you were referred by someone in the prospect company's office. Remember: At this point, you are only looking for information.

For example, if you are selling copiers, you want to learn if this office has problems with the toner or paper jams. If so, how long does it take to get a replacement or fix the problem? Ask to make a copy of something for yourself. If the copy is gray, ask when the copier was last serviced. Are they happy with the quality of the copies and how quickly problems are corrected? Do they find that copies are black or smudged?

If an office seems unhappy with the present product, contact the buyer. Remember to only ask questions to which you know the answer. Most buyers want to get rid of salespeople, so a seemingly ingenuous offer to go away may work. In the case of the copier, Spokes suggests a question such as, "Have you ever noticed that if you run copies, they may be gray instead of black?" (You already know this.) "If this isn't a problem, I'm probably wasting your time. But if it is, we need to talk. Can we run off a copy?"

Spokes and his reps use another untraditional strategy to find advertising prospects. They read newspaper headlines and identify organizations likely to strongly agree or disagree with the message. Then they contact those organizations and invite them to get their message out through an ad.

Staples Business Expo sales representative Sean Smith, in Stevens, Pennsylvania, sells digital imaging to businesses. Smith has three suggestions for businesses serving a local community or area:

1. Join your local Chamber of Commerce and buy its membership list.

2. Volunteer in your community. A volunteer who is a real-estate agent becomes known as the person to see when you think about selling your home.

3. Advertise in your local church or community newsletter. Smith recalls, "A friend of mine started his own construction business 10 years ago. After two difficult months, he placed business-card ads in his local church bulletin. People saw his ad and asked his advice. Now he has 15 to 20 people working for him."

If your customer base is regional, Smith recommends consulting telephone directories in areas you visit, purchasing subscriber lists from industrywide magazines serving your potential market, and using lead-generation companies such as infoUSA.

Once you have identified potential customers, visit each company's Web site. Learn when the company started, identify its chief officers, and read the company's goals and mission and its annual report (if available), as well as any other information that may help you use your products or services to solve one of its needs or problems.

Spokes adds these tips: Identify the demographics (age, gender, geographic area, etc.) of your users, match needs with what you offer, and understand why people might purchase your product or service. In a competitive market, the only new sales may be replacement sales.

When following up with leads, Smith emphasizes, "You are selling a solution to a customer's needs."

Do your homework and take the time to grow, develop, and qualify potential leads. Your sales success will increase as prospects choose you as their preferred product or service provider.

SEVEN TIPS FOR QUALIFYING

The following tips were provided by Myers Barnes, president of Myers Barnes Associates, a consulting and sales coaching firm

Your goal in professional selling is straightforward: Determine the customer's needs, offer solutions, and successfully conclude the transaction as soon as possible. This necessitates qualifying prospects. Here are seven reasons why it is essential to qualify your prospects.

1. **Qualifying determines wants, needs, and desires:** It is a process of discovery. Once you discover there is a distinct need that can be fulfilled by your product or service, take steps toward committing time and energy.

2. **Qualifying provides you with the prospect's financial status:** If you find that there is a need, your next priority is to determine whether the prospect has adequate funds available to fill it.

3. **Qualifying provides you with the prospect's financial parameters:** In order to develop an appropriate solution to a problem, you need to have an idea of the prospect's budget. If you present a $1,000 solution to a $10,000 need, you'll only frustrate the prospect and lose the sale.

4. **Qualifying determines all parties involved in the decision:** There's nothing more frustrating than knocking somebody's socks off with a dynamic presentation only to find out that the sale is contingent on someone else.

5. **Qualifying determines the time frame:** It's essential that you know when the prospect is willing to take advantage of your offer—whether it's today, next week, next month, or next year.

6. **Qualifying reveals the competition:** When you qualify you find out who your competitors are.

7. **Qualifying helps eliminate objections before they appear:** If you question skillfully and listen attentively, prospective purchasers will tell you everything you need to know to help them with their buying decisions.

CHAPTER 10

Relationship Building

USING RELATIONSHIP BUILDING TO GET MORE OUT OF YOUR BEST ACCOUNTS

Sales professionals are always looking for ways to maximize and economize at the same time; today sales are an even bigger challenge than usual. One way to maximize sales while economizing on the expense of developing new accounts is to get more from the best of your customer base. If you do it right, you'll help your customers while you're helping yourself.

To learn how professional salespeople make the most of their best accounts, follow the advice of Michael Pisarski, who handles corporate sales for Bay to Bay Hardware and Pool Supplies in Tampa, Florida, and of Cecil Carder, regional sales manager for Havel, Giarusso and Associates Inc. in Olathe, Kansas. Pisarski says that making the most of his best customers means examining the 20 percent of his business that accounts for 80 percent of his sales.

"We're located in a very vibrant business community," Pisarski says. "But as the economy began to tighten, we realized that we needed to do more with less. That meant we needed to really listen to our customers."

Pisarski says that salespeople who have worked in one field for a long time tend to make sales assumptions that work against their giving the best service possible and getting the most out of their accounts.

"I've probably heard every possible plumbing problem that a client can encounter," he says. "Because of that, I'd gotten into the habit of mentally pricing the job out for my contractors as soon as they told me what type of job they were doing; in other words, I'd stopped listening. But in this economy I've gone back to really listening to the job order and asking more follow-up questions. As a result, I'm picking up an additional 10 to 15 percent in parts orders from our core clients, not by forcing a sale, but by doing the job the way it should be done all the time. It makes me wonder why it took a slowdown to make me do things I knew I should be doing all along."

Carder says it takes a long time to develop an account to the point where you can get the most out of it. "Never lose sight of the fact that the client is always in control," he says. "But over time, if you can get to know a client and build a relationship with him away from the business, you develop a business relationship on a totally different level. That gives you some control over the account, as opposed to being in the store for an hour or two, where all you can do is make a presentation."

Carder tries to spend time with clients on outings that range from a simple meal away from the business to a several-day hunting camp. These longer outings, he says, help create an atmosphere where most of the business for the year can sometimes be set up. Since Carder sells outdoor products related to hunting, putting products into his clients' hands in the field has potential to increase his sales.

"Any hands-on experience with a product gives the customer a sense of ownership in that product line," he says. "When a retailer feels a sense of ownership in a specific line, he orders more of it. This helps creates a sense of partnership between the retailer and us, so that now his inventory-control issues become our inventory-control issues as well. We have an obligation to keep his inventory of our products at a level that will give him the markup he expects."

Taking the time to build relationships also creates trust, which can lead to increased sales, Carder says. "Because the customer trusts us, over time we can increase the sale of items he hasn't previously carried," he says. "When you have that type of relationship with the guy across the table, where he knows you aren't going to just throw something at him that doesn't fit with his plan, you gain credibility.

"Sometimes I walk into a sales situation and put a product out on the desk and never say anything about it. At some time during the conversation the customer may ask about that product, and then the process begins. Is it right for the store at this time? Are the margins right? What about support? The retailer may also let me know that there's floor or shelf space for that product. That helps as well, because now I have a better idea of what kind of products to show him or not to show him."

When you're working with your best accounts, Carder says, never forget that the customer's needs always override your need to make additional sales. "It's not worth putting a trusting relationship with a long-term sales partner at risk just to push an additional sale through. Trusting each other is essential to building a long-term relationship that will be profitable for everyone concerned."

RELATIONSHIP-BUILDING SKILL SET

1. Find out which 20 percent of your customers make up 80 percent of your business.

2. Don't assume; listen to what your customers really need.

3. Ask follow-up questions.

4. Spend time developing personal relationships with customers, which leads to trust.

5. Give clients hands-on experience with products where possible.

6. Don't risk long-term trusting relationships for short-term increased sales.

7. Keep notes on clients' personal information, and use that information to help develop relationships.

8. Get to know clients away from business.

TIPS TO BUILDING RAPPORT WITH YOUR CUSTOMERS

As a diligent sales professional, you're always striving to break down the barriers between you and your clients. The key to tearing down those walls in customer relationships is building rapport. Get close enough to your customers, as the saying goes, and you can slow-dance together as long as the music plays. Richard Buckingham, author of *Customer Once, Client Forever* suggests the following rapport-building tips:

1. **Go the extra smile:** Smiling is extremely important when you're face-to-face with the customer, but it's also critical when you're talking on the phone. Before picking up the receiver, think about all the value you can bring to this customer. If that doesn't put a smile on your face, perhaps you shouldn't be calling in the first place.

2. **Dig for common ground:** Before meeting with a new prospect, research both the contact's business and personal interests. Looks for areas of commonality—do you share an interest in sports, a hobby, background, the arts, movies, and so on? Common interests can provide a powerful icebreaker and help the relationship bound ahead in ways that talking business can't.

3. **Undivide your attention:** You know it's important to listen carefully and actively to clients—a very difficult task when you face frequent interruptions. Before a meeting, let the customer know you are turning off your pager, beeper, cell phone, and so on; closing your door; and holding all your telephone calls. This sets the tone

that you plan on paying close attention to everything he or she has to say.

4. **Join the agree club:** When a customer offers up an opinion that you share, go ahead and express your agreement: "I couldn't agree more." But when the situation is reversed, don't be as quick to disagree. Disagreement at the outset of a relationship is a rapport killer. Instead, look for areas where you are in accord, or try to see things from the customer's view. Use expressions like "I agree with you that," "I appreciate your point that . . . ." or "You have an interesting point there."

CREATIVE WAYS TO STAND OUT FROM THE CROWD

With all the other salespeople vying for your prospects' attention, to stand a chance of getting the sale, you must find ways to shine. The following ideas will help you make an unforgettable impression on your prospects so they remember you when it's time to buy:

1. **Make their special occasions memorable:** Helping your prospects celebrate their special days with a simple card or gift helps build trust by showing you care. One sales professional sent a birthday card to a video store owner who had never bought from him, and he signed a long-term contract with that company the same day. Apparently, no one else had remembered his birthday. Personalize all your greetings with a handwritten note, and include cartoons or articles that may interest your prospect.

2. **Establish curiosity:** Once a month, one salesperson takes his pet pig and makes calls on prospects with whom he's been unable to get an appointment. He gets in almost every time and makes a truly unforgettable appearance. With a little imagination, you should be able to do the same. Offer lottery tickets to prospects who will "take a chance" and meet with you, or make trivia questions part of your presentation and offer a small prize for each correct answer your buyer gives. Anything that makes prospects give you a second look can help you get an appointment.

3. **Learn your buyers' interests:** Careful listening and observation should clue you in to a few of your buyer's favorite things. On your next visit, bring an issue of a magazine or some other small gift related to those interests. If your buyer seems to enjoy telling jokes when you come to call, ask around for some good jokes before your next appointment. By taking an interest in your buyer's interests, you should be able to build rapport and earn sales more easily.

4. **Build emotional rapport:** What concerns your buyer should concern you. Many buyers might just enjoy the chance to unload for a little while on their prospects. Always to be willing to listen to your buyer's troubles and take a sincere interest in helping out. Another salesperson once had a client who owned a farm, and on every call they talked about the farm before they got down to business. Two months after the salesperson was promoted and someone else took over the account, the buyer took his business elsewhere. Buyers want to know you care before they hand over an order.

5. **Go out on a limb:** If you've been calling on a prospect for months without success, you've got little to lose by trying a more unorthodox approach. Again, creativity is key. Question the prospect's secretary or coworkers to find out his or her pet peeves and personal preferences. Use what you know to make a bolder attempt at an appointment. If you find out that your buyer likes a certain musical artist, try singing a voice mail message to one of that artist's popular tunes. Billionaire Ted Turner wasn't too proud to drop to his knees and tell stubborn clients, "You're killing me!" to persuade them to buy. Even if your attempts don't succeed, at least you'll know you tried everything.

HOW TO REPAIR TROUBLED CUSTOMER RELATIONSHIPS

No matter how hard you work, inevitably something will throw a monkey wrench into the near-perfect customer relationships you've developed. According to Mark Dixon, sales manager for Legacy Custom Builders in Scottsdale, Arizona, when handled properly, a snafu can actually build a customer's confidence in you and your company and strengthen the relationship's long-term prospects. Here are Dixon's five tips for handling situations that go awry.

1. **Be up-front:** "Set the customer's expectation level by saying at the outset, 'During this project, unexpected things will happen. We don't know what they are, but when we make a mistake, rest assured we will take care of it.' Then if nothing does go wrong, you've exceeded expectations and customers will rave about you."

2. **Mistakes mean having to say you're sorry:** "When trouble crops up, the most important thing is to acknowledge accountability. It doesn't matter whether you're responsible for it or even if you feel the client played a role. Say, 'We're sorry, you're right. What we did was wrong' or 'You weren't appreciated as much as you should be.'"

3. **Change is good:** "It's one thing to say you're sorry and to tell a client that the mistake won't happen again. Even better is to go a step farther and explain what policies you'll put in place to guarantee it won't. You want the opportunity to show the customer that this mistake is not indicative of how you run your organization."

4. **Ask not what your customer has done to you:** "Keep the lines of communication open. We do this by scheduling weekly meetings with clients while we're remodeling their homes. We follow an agenda and the last question is always, 'How are we performing?' We want to know the good, the bad, and the ugly. It lets clients know you care about what they think and how you're doing, and it also gets problems out in the open before they can blow it out of proportion."

5. **Managers, keep out:** "When you have to address problems, it's best for customers to hear it from the reps they've been dealing with. It's tempting for a manager to try to step in to clean up the mess, but it's much better for the reps to step up, take responsibility, and show the customers their integrity. The manager's role is to be honest with the reps, discuss ways to handle the situation, and then let them go back and take care of the customers."

CHAPTER 11

Getting Past Gatekeepers

YOUR ALLY, THE GATEKEEPER

Are gatekeepers problems or partners? It depends on how you approach them, says Jeff Blackman, a business-growth specialist. "If you treat gatekeepers as subservient individuals and then ask for the decision maker, you won't get anywhere," he says. "The key is to make gatekeepers your allies. Use them as advisors. Let them know you respect their job."

First impressions often make a lasting impression when it comes to dealing with gatekeepers. That's why it's important to be considerate as well as enthusiastic. Be knowledgeable about both your product and the company on which you are calling. If you come across as unprepared, phony, or obnoxious, it may lock the gate. Look at it from the gatekeeper's perspective— what type of person do you like to deal with?

"Sometimes it's the most simplistic and most sensible things that yield the greatest results. Be nice, be courteous, and seek their counsel," says Blackman.

"If you make cold calls, and I don't recommend them, there is a set of rules that you need to follow," says Blackman, who advises his clients to use referrals instead of cold calls. "First and foremost, look at gatekeepers as strategic advisors and providers of information. Begin by telling them how you have helped similar organizations solve similar problems and generate specific results. Ask such questions as, could you help me out? What can you tell me about your organization and how you've used X in the past? Most of the time, people will be glad to help you."

Another way you can make it easier on yourself, says Blackman, is to e-mail the decision maker ahead of time. You can get e-mail addresses from company Web sites or by asking receptionists. Then when you call, you can use the e-mail as a point of reference with the gatekeeper. It also helps to know the gatekeeper's name.

Here are some other tips from Blackman: Call during off-hours (gatekeepers usually work nine to five), and know the name of the person you want to talk to. Don't just ask for the decision maker. Finally, don't think of gatekeepers as your enemies or people to avoid; think of them as your aides and people who can assist you in your quest to get the sale.

APPOINTMENT-SETTING TIPS

In his book *Successful Cold Call Selling*, Lee Boyan offers appointment-setting tips to set you up for more sales, plus his favorite appointment clincher:

"Mr. Prospect, I wouldn't begin to tell you that you need what I have. That is for you to decide. But I guarantee you will get enough profitable ideas from our interview to make it well worth 30 minutes of your time. Can we do that on [first choice of date] or would [second choice] be better?"

If you still meet with resistance:

1. **Listen carefully:** Resist the urge to cut your prospects off. Listen for their emotions and use them to plan your responses.

2. **Restate ambiguous language:** If your prospects try to brush you off or hide a need, paraphrase them more clearly, and end your statement by asking, "Am I understanding you correctly?"

3. **Don't ask whether your prospects will see you, ask when:** Offer a choice of two dates in the very near future.

GET YOUR FOOT IN THE DOOR: 11 APPOINTMENT-SETTING TECHNIQUES THAT KEEP YOU IN FRONT OF CUSTOMERS

Not every call you make will end in a sale, but to even get a chance to close, you need an appointment with the decision maker. The stiffer the competition for your prospect's time, the more important it is to get your foot in the door before your competition does. To get your prospects to take you seriously, convince them that an appointment with you is time well spent.

These 11 tips will help you understand what to say and how to say it to get the appointments that help increase sales.

1. **Start tearing down buyer barriers immediately:** To help you avoid being shut out by a wary gatekeeper, plan your greeting carefully. Politely identify yourself and your product or service. Use a friendly tone and impeccable phone manners to set you apart from the other salespeople who call on your prospect.

2. **Be creative:** An off-the-wall approach might throw a difficult gatekeeper temporarily off guard—just be careful not to say anything that might hurt your chances of getting an audience with your prospect.

3. **Earn the receptionist's favor:** In many cases the receptionist decides who will and won't get an appointment with your prospect. To make sure the receptionists you reach are on your side, treat them with respect. Ask for and use their names to show them that you view them as people and not just as petty annoyances standing between you and your prospects. If you treat receptionists like the VIPs they are, they may be more likely to treat you like one. When you've collected the information you need, thank the receptionist warmly by name before you get transferred or hang up.

4. **Tear down buyer barriers with your prospects:** Start building rapport from the moment you get through to your prospect. Ask open-ended questions that encourage buyers to talk and help you analyze their needs. Use words such as "may," "might," and "could," for example, and such phrases as "an opportunity you may find interesting"

or "a plan that could cultivate new customers." If you establish yourself as a trustworthy, knowledgeable, and caring person before you start talking about your product, your prospect may listen more carefully—and buy more quickly.

5. **Appeal to the buyer's best interests:** To pinpoint your buyer's specific needs, do some homework before you make your first call. Make a brief but powerful benefits statement that grabs your prospect's attention and whets the appetite for more information. Instead of giving a long boring list of your product's bells and whistles, reassure your prospect that his or her needs come first by outlining how your product can meet those needs.

6. **Answer the buyer's unasked question, "What's in it for me?"** Briefly outline how your product could meet your prospect's needs, then show how that affects your prospect personally. If your product could help reduce your buyer's workload or help impress top-level management, say so. When you talk to your buyer, instead of using the phrases "your company's profits" or "your department's productivity," give your words more personal impact by saying "your profits" and "your productivity."

7. **Appeal to the buyer's sense of reason and emotion:** Some prospects base buying decisions on logic; others go with feelings and emotions. You might not be able to tell how your buyer makes decisions in the short time you have, so use a little of both to get the appointment. For the logical decision maker, use concise, rational arguments that emphasize the measurable positive results of using your

product. To win over the emotional decision maker, use image-building language and emphasize how product benefits will make the prospect feel (e.g., "Won't it feel great not to worry about production delays anymore?").

8. **Establish the offer's credibility:** If your prospect believes there's a sucker born every minute, you have to show that buying from you is safe and smart. Establish credibility by gathering facts and figures to back up your claims. To make a positive impression on a wary prospect, for example, you might say, "XYZ Company used this product to decrease their product defects by 23 percent." This statement boosts your credibility by providing specific information on what your product can do and giving the name of a company prospects can call to verify it. Tell the buyer that you have a collection of testimonials from other satisfied customers.

9. **Show respect for the buyer's time:** Tell prospects exactly how much time the appointment will take, and emphasize that you know their time is valuable. Keep your conversation brief—save your product presentation for the appointment. Use words that make it clear that you're trying to take up as little of their time as possible: "I'd like to very quickly tell you about this opportunity," or "May I take a moment to discuss this with you briefly?" Your efforts to save the prospect's time help prove that you sincerely care about your customers.

10. **Reassure buyers that when you meet with them you'll provide all the information they need to make a decision:** Your statement will help reassure them that you'll tell

them everything they need to know, so they won't have to conduct any personal research to confirm your product's value or your credibility. Emphasize that you want them to make an educated, informed decision and that the material you bring will allow them to do that. You might also shorten the buying cycle by suggesting that since they'll have all the information they need right in front of them, they'll be able to make a prompt and wise decision.

11. **Confirm the appointment:** Send a brief, handwritten note with the date, time, and place of your appointment. Enclose your business card and an article that may interest the prospect, or maybe some product literature that addresses concerns raised when you arranged your meeting. On the day before your appointment, call again to make sure the decision maker is still able to meet you at the prearranged time.

Markets are so competitive and your buyers are often so busy that just getting an appointment—never mind a sale—takes an edge. By creating a strong first impression, you can give yourself the chance to tell your prospects about your product or service. A proven appointment-setting strategy can help give you greater access to prospects and sales.

CHAPTER 12

Beating the Competition

THE CHALLENGE OF YOUR COMPETITION

How do you view your competition? Are they a threat or are they a challenge?

Akio Morita, a Japanese businessman, had formed a company called Tokyo Telecommunications. His company's main product had been tape recorders, but with the advent of transistors, the product line had been expanded to include radios and televisions. The market in Japan was too small for Morita; he wanted to export. As he traveled around the world, most countries either prohibited him from bringing his products into the country or placed so many restrictions on the transaction that it would not be profitable to Tokyo Telecommunications. These countries were afraid that the competition from Morita's company would harm the domestic manufacturers.

One country allowed Morita to market his products. About the people of this country Morita said, "I admire their confidence in their own abilities." The country was the United States. Morita renamed his company so people could remember it. He called it "Sony."

The influence of Sony in the American marketplace caused the innovative manufacturers of electronic equipment to become even better. It caused the weaker companies to complain.

Sony had taken the transistor, an idea pioneered by Bell Labs, and had used it to build a multimillion-dollar market. Sony had used its strength in marketing to succeed with someone else's idea.

How do you respond to competition? Do you try to put it down or find ways to prevent it? Or do you try to find ways to capitalize on it?

Everyone learns from the competition. Some people learn how to improve; others learn how to lose gracefully. Some want to be the only kid on the block, others want to be the best kid on the block. If nothing else, your competition will reveal what kind of person you are.

Remember, you cannot hold a person down unless you're willing to stay down with him or her. Grow with your competition, and allow them to be the absolute best that they can be. And then, be just a little bit better yourself.

TIPS FOR LURING CUSTOMERS AWAY FROM THE COMPETITION

Satisfied customers are reluctant to switch suppliers. This works great for the accounts you've already won, but it can make earning new business frustrating and time-consuming. According to David Emmons, sales manager with Electric Melting Services in Anniston, Alabama, the recipe for winning business away from competitors requires attitude, perseverance, and information gathering.

While Emmons may hate visiting a prospect 10 times in six months with nothing to show for the effort, he channels those feelings into finding a better way. "I find those accounts a challenge. You should always go by and see them and make an attempt to get in, no matter what's happened in the past. Keep your face in front of them until the opportunity arises to make your move."

In these cases, Emmons says, opportunity typically arrives when the competition stumbles or takes an account for granted. "When something goes wrong it means the competitor probably betrayed a trust on some level or promised something they couldn't deliver," he notes. "That's why you keep calling, in the hopes that you'll hit the prospect when trouble arises with the current supplier. At some point the competition will slip up. That's the best opportunity to get in, make the presentation, and prove to the customer that you can beat what the current supplier is offering."

Emmons adds, however, that winning business from the competition isn't a completely passive operation. Whenever possible, he tries to forge ties with colleagues in related industries who might provide tips when a competitor has failed to deliver for a customer.

"I have business associates who work in our industry, but who aren't competitors," Emmons says. "Because of that established relationship, they may give me a heads-up about a possible opportunity, saying 'We were at so-and-so's plant and a failure occurred.' That way I know the time is ripe to make a call on that competitor's customer. It's not exactly espionage, but it is an effective way to keep your ear to the ground."

HEAD OFF THE COMPETITION

You probably feel very comfortable dealing with your long-term customers. They've been with you for years and are dependable for a solid piece of business. Through good times and bad, you know these clients will stick with you. Or will they? Paradoxically, your most reliable customers also may be the most likely to jump ship, concerned that you have begun to take them for granted. But not to worry. In *Unleashing Business Creativity*, author Bill Peters suggests the following effective exercise for anticipating and heading off competitive challenges:

1. Identify your four primary competitors.

2. Divide your team into four groups. Have each group represent one competitor and come up with possible three- and five-year plans for the future.

3. Bring the entire team together to review the four plans. Brainstorm your company's best Plan A and Plan B for addressing these competitive challenges.

4. Again as a group, imagine two new competitors (not in the original four) and consider what their three- and five-year plans might be.

5. Refine your Plans A and B to address these challenges as well, and add a Plan C.

6. Discuss the key assumptions, necessary resources, and personnel involved in your three plans. Settle on the one alternative that is most reasonable and consistent with your company mission.

Challenge this thinking every year to make sure you are following through as effectively as possibly on your planning. Rethink the entire strategy every three years.

COMPETITION CAN BE YOUR WINNING GAME

No matter what you sell, the competition is out there selling too! By using smart strategies, you can handle competition, while strengthening your customer base and increasing your sales. Use the following four rules to help you deal effectively with your major competitors:

1. **Rule 1: Respect your competition:** Avoid attacking your competitor's business or products. Never make any personal attacks. That kind of behavior will damage your integrity.

   Never criticize your prospect for considering doing business with your competitor. If you do, your prospect may think you are questioning his or her intelligence. This can make your prospects angry, even though they may not tell you in so many words.

2. **Rule 2: Know your competition:** Know what claims your competitors are making about their products. Are they true? If not, you can handle the situation during your sales presentation without ever mentioning your competitors' products.

Learn your competitors' vulnerable points. Capitalize on their weaknesses during your presentation by stressing points about your product that you know they can't match. When doing this, you don't have to mention your competitors by name.

Know what negative claims your competitors are making about your product. Apply "criteria selling" techniques—you set the standard for the industry. Cover all the points in your presentation that you know the product provides, and show how your product meets this criteria. You can neutralize their negative claims without mentioning your competitors.

Learn how far along your competitor is in the sales process. Use open-ended questions (how, who, what, when, why) with your prospects. The more you know about your prospect's consideration of the competition, the better you will handle the situation.

3. **Rule 3: Sell your own product:** Always show how your product is better, not how your competitor's is worse. It's hard to gain credibility and sustain your integrity when you are running down your competitor's product. After all, it may be as good as yours.

    Emphasize those features and benefits that your competitor can't match. Concentrate on the benefits and show how each benefit relates directly to helping your prospect achieve his or her goals.

4. **Rule 4: Show your prospect that you care:** The biggest edge you can get on your competitor is to care about your prospect. Remember that prospects don't care how

much you know until they know how much you care. If you change the first letter of the word "sell" to "h" and the last letter to "p," you get the word "help." And this is the answer to successful selling.

If you are there to help, you are doing something *for* them. Your prospects can quickly tell the difference. Stop selling ... start helping! You have to care about your prospects to keep them from turning to the competition.

CHAPTER 13

Uncovering Needs

WHAT DOES YOUR CUSTOMER WANT?

To operate at full potential on a sales call, salespeople know they have to participate fully in the moment, actively listening to the customer, processing information, and asking thoughtful follow-up questions that lead to greater mutual understanding and build relationships. But according to noted business coach and speaker Keith Rosen, too frequently salespeople drift out of the present and away from the immediacy of the sales call at hand.

If you're not living in the present, then where are you? Rosen says that many salespeople let their minds wander to the end of the call as they begin thinking about the outcome and whether they will make a sale. If your mind is on the future, he notes, it can't be focusing on what the customer is saying.

Rosen also recognizes that salespeople frequently allow customer objections to take them out of the moment and into the past. An objection may shift you into survival mode, he says, where you reflect on similar situations you've faced and where you act out the same counterproductive patterns that have failed you in the past.

To remain engaged and in the present, even in the face of a customer objection, Rosen suggests salespeople replace reactive behaviors–where you act without thinking–with responsive behaviors.

For example, when a customer utters those six deadly words, "I'll have to think about it," the reactive salesperson typically becomes flustered and responds with a "but" statement:

- But our company's service is . . .

- But this is a great price.

- But we have the best products in the industry.

- But think about the value we offer.

The responsive salesperson, on the other hand, comes back at the customer with an open-ended probing question that maintains the dialogue and keeps the information flowing:

- Why do you feel that way?

- What benefits do you see from this course of action?

- What is missing from this solution to make you more comfortable?

- What is a better approach to this dilemma?

- I'm not sure I understand. Can you explain further?

With such follow-up questions, you remain focused on the moment at hand and return the issue to customers, who will either convince themselves to buy after all or will at least share with you the actual reasons why they aren't buying from you today.

FOUR KEY LISTENING TIPS TO UNCOVER CUSTOMERS NEEDS

1. **Concentrate:** Pay 100 percent attention to everything your customer says. Focus on the buyer's body language, note the tone of voice, watch the client's hands.

2. **Clarify:** Many clients use buzzwords, insider language, or abbreviations that you may not be familiar with. Never be afraid to reveal your ignorance. Ask questions quickly so you can avoid costly misunderstandings later.

3. **Rephrase:** Verify your understanding with phrases like: "To help me stay on course, allow me to summarize my understanding of this situation..." or "Allow me to put this in my own words..." or "Let me just restate briefly...."

4. **Write down key ideas:** Salespeople who take notes won't forget important details. These notes come in handy a few days later when you're back in the office developing your proposal.

TIPS FOR EXPOSING THE CUSTOMER NEEDS THAT LEAD TO SALES OPPORTUNITIES

As an Anheuser-Busch beer distributor operating in Washington state, Kevin Dykman needs to do more than sell beer to his customers. He has to help his customers move the product off their shelves as well. To do so effectively, Dykman says he first has to gain his customers' trust and ask questions that determine the challenges they face. To ferret out real customer issues and concerns, Dykman suggests the following strategies:

1. **Manage top down:** "With some of my customers, for example, at the supermarket level, it can be difficult to determine who the decision maker actually is. We try to begin with the store manager and ask who should make decisions about store displays. But even if that person delegates authority, he will often overrule an assistant manager's decision. So keeping up communication is very important. The best policy is to get as high as you can at the point you're at. It's easier to work your way down than up."

2. **Be a harsh *ask* master:** "When you ask customers how things are going, they'll often respond with 'Fine.' It's natural. But then if you ask again, 'Are you really fine? I notice your draft beer sales are down. Any idea why that is?' then all of a sudden they start opening up. You shouldn't be satisfied with a pat answer. Let customers know you really care about what's going on, and ask as many times as necessary to communicate that."

3. **Expose the need:** "To help customers you have to know how they want to do business. In our industry that means finding out how they want to make money. Do they want higher profits? More total sales? More returns for less profit? Some customers would rather sell fewer cases but make large margins on them, whereas others just want to sell the hell out of the stuff. How customers

want to make money affects how we can help them price their entire beer cooler."

4. **May the source be with you:** "Sometimes customers don't even understand they're facing a problem, and we have to shed light on the situation. Other times, they're just at a loss and we can offer help with our knowledge and experience. Recently, one of our customers was competing with a large chain store that opened up nearby. We suggested that he try something different— putting banners up with one hot item and running a deal for two weeks at a time. He was sort of giving up the fight, but we were able to encourage him not to, and we suggested angles he could use to win customers back."

5. **Run the options:** "We have a paid performance plan. A lot of it is incentive work, and each month we'll set up a certain item to get into stores. But we found that if we highlight only one item per month, then that may not be the best solution for every customer. You wind up encouraging salespeople to be pushing the same thing on everyone. So now we have three different special items a month, and salespeople have more leeway in determining the best match. But there is no one-size-fits-all solution that will work with all accounts."

THINK LIKE YOUR CUSTOMER

Wouldn't it be great if you could just open up your customers' brains and root around in there to see what they're thinking? Unfortunately, they tend to back away as soon as you break out the scalpel. So what's the next best thing? Asking the right questions. And no one knows more about how to issue deal-making queries than author Charles Brennan. In *Sales Questions that Close the Sale: How to Uncover Your Customers' Real Needs*, Brennan offers the following tips:

1. **Pipe down:** After you ask a customer a question, remain silent. Let the customer think. If your question is a good one, you shouldn't have to break the silence first.

2. **Once is enough:** Perhaps surprisingly, salespeople frequently repeat questions, typically out of nervousness. Needless to say, this makes a poor impression on customers. Solution: Write your questions down and check them off as you go.

3. **Put it to the group:** When you're faced with a team of buyers, avoid directing your questions at the one person you believe is the decision maker. First, your assumption could be wrong. Second, the person you ignore today may be in a power position tomorrow. Best not to char that bridge around the edges. Third, it's plain impolite. Besides, you want everyone to understand the need for change, and that means engaging the group.

4. **What's that you say?** You may love the sound of your own voice, but you're asking questions to get answers. Listen to them. Don't let your mind wander. It's unbelievable how often this seemingly obvious rule is violated. Don't think of your next question while the prospect is talking.

5. **Have more at the ready:** Despite the previous tip, you should be prepared to ask follow-up questions.

Be prepared—ahead of time—with questions that relate to the customers' key issues, whether cost containment, productivity, profitability, or competitive pressure. But make sure your product or service can address the issue you're asking about.

CHAPTER 14

How to Sell Value

SELL VALUE BEFORE YOU QUOTE PRICE

For decades, sales experts have taught salespeople to sell everything first and give the price last. But no matter how well you try to sell the benefits of your product, you will still have prospects who want to know the price early in the presentation. Some will object to your price, no matter how many benefits your product may have for them. These guidelines are good ones to follow when handling questions and objections on price.

When a customer asks early in the presentation, "How much does it cost?" a good response is, "It really depends on the options you select. Let me explain our investment structure to you in a moment. Now earlier you said that you wanted . . . ." This takes your customer's mind off price and gives you the opportunity to relate more product benefits to his or her wants and needs.

A customer who bargains for a lower price is most often better served by converting price quotes from a total investment figure (total dollars) to a monthly investment figure (monthly dollars). A smaller monthly investment is easier to accept than a large-figure total investment.

When you are quoting a price, it is a good idea to follow up by stating the benefits (immediate, long-term, or competitive edge) that a customer will receive. One recommendation is to state money quotations without tax and delivery charges. In addition, it is a good idea to avoid using the word "dollars" because it can strike fear in a buyer when he or she hears it related to spending. For example, say: "This model is only 750 and it includes...." However, do use the word "dollars" when showing customers a savings. For example: "With this option you can save $75!"

Use phrases that minimize price resistance: "Your return includes..."; "The value you will receive will be..."; "You get this..."; "Your investment is only..." Buyers have reflexes, too. The word "cost" or "price" can cause people to think that it costs too much or the price is too high.

Use tie-downs throughout your presentation to gain the customer's agreement. Tie-down techniques lead customers to establish a pattern of yes responses. They are used to feed back information obtained during the qualification process. The sales adage "When a customer says it, it's always the truth!" applies here. Tie-downs reiterate to the customer what he or she had told you. "You did say...," or, "As you said earlier..."

Introduce prices in ranges. Any price is more easily sold when it is part of a price range. The choice of having three investment ranges allows customers to prepare themselves for a decision.

Instead of lowering your price, offer an earlier delivery date, a company gift, and so on. Write down what's been conceded because, unless you keep track, it's nearly impossible to determine whether or not the give-and-take is working both ways.

Keep your distance! Maintain a mystique by not becoming too friendly until they commit to your figure.

The bigger the sale, the bigger the chance the buyer will be tempted to ask for a lower price. When a customer objects to your price, the right words, the right voice inflection suggesting the right product, and the right intent will persuade many price objectors to buy from you.

HOW TO ADD VALUE TO EVERY SALES CALL

A salesperson's skill can add as much as 50 percent to the perceived value of any product or service. In many cases, particularly in service-based industries, it can add much more. A high-quality and professional approach is a powerful way to add value and differentiate yourself from your competitors.

Many top consulting firms carefully groom and train their senior consultants, knowing that how clients perceive them is as important as the work they carry out. Everything you do is either increasing your perceived value or detracting from it. Intangible and imperceptible details may have the biggest potential to influence your customer's perception of quality.

Here are 10 ways to increase your "perceived value rating":

1. **Be well dressed:** Most business people respect conservative attire more than fashion dressing. Make sure your clothes are well fitting and neatly pressed.

2. **Invest in expensive or good-quality accessories:** These include your pen, watch, briefcase, and so on.

3. **Have a tidy, neat, well-groomed appearance:** Customers will appreciate your attention to details.

4. **Practice impeccable manners, politeness, and courtesy:** Put your best self forward, all the time and to everyone.

5. **Never knock the competition:** If you do, you decrease your own value.

6. **Be on time and deliver everything you promise:** You are building your own reputation.

7. **Never argue with customers:** They may not always be right, but they are always the customers.

8. **Look for opportunities to do something extra:** Little things mean a lot.

9. **Plan and prepare each appointment in advance:** Don't leave things to chance or try to wing it.

10. **Write thank-you notes to each new customer or prospect:** It is practically free to say thank you!

BOTTOM-LINE BENEFITS

One of the surest ways to add real value in the mind of the customer is to focus your sales presentation around bottom-line benefits. Everybody, whether buying for personal or business reasons, can relate to these high-value criteria:

■ Saving money

■ Saving time (which is money)

■ Improving satisfaction and quality levels

Build a simple model into every sales presentation to help prospects cost-justify your product or service, showing specific, quantifiable savings in time or money over alternative solutions.

Always make sure that your sales approach adds value by developing the most important bottom-line benefits— features your customers can measure in terms of improving quality above what they now have, or how your products and/or services can help save or make them time or money.

CHAPTER 15

Fearless Presentations

PRESENTATION POLISH

Whether you're addressing your sales team or a meeting room of million-dollar prospects, good speaking and presentation skills are essential to sales success. Even the most seasoned sales veterans sometimes feel shaky about making important presentations in front of a group. If the idea of speaking to more than one other person makes your knees knock and your heart race, try these hints to take your orations from panicked to polished.

Preparation

Before you prepare your presentation, make sure that you thoroughly research both your subject and your audience. Tailor your presentation to audience needs and interests.

Structure your speech or presentation carefully with an introduction, strategically ordered main points, and a conclusion.
For example, you may make a longer lasting impression by
presenting your most compelling arguments last, then ending
with a strong and persuasive summary of your most important
points.

To prepare mentally, envision yourself being introduced,
taking the floor and addressing the group smoothly and elo-
quently. A lectern may make you feel less exposed and more
comfortable if you are speaking from a stage or platform. If
you need one, use a microphone. If you are making a presentation to a group of buyers, you may want to use a laptop computer to enhance your presentation with images that put some
color and motion into your subject. Before you make your presentation, record your speech with a tape recorder or a video
camera. A videotape will show you how your gestures and
mannerisms emphasize—or undermine—your words. Study
the videotape of your speech and record it over until you are
happy with the result.

At the Lectern

When your moment arrives, take a few deep breaths to relax.
Walk briskly to the lectern, thank your host, and proceed with
confidence. Use these tips as a guide to making your presentation as professional and smooth as possible.

- Do not staple script or notes together. Number speech
  pages, and when reading, slide the completed page

across to reveal the next one. If you maintain eye contact with the audience, they probably won't notice the turning pages.

- Do not pick up or shuffle papers, or fidget with clothing, pencil, or pen. If you must refer to your notes, drop your eyes—not your head. Keep your head aimed at the audience.

- Maintain eye contact with your audience, shifting your focus from one interested party to the next.

- Don't lean on the lectern, grasp or clutch the sides, or lock your arms folded across your chest.

- Gesture naturally. Gestures above the shoulder line look false. Keep your hands at your sides—if you have problems with nervous gestures, rest one hand on the side of the lectern and one at your side or in a pants pocket.

Although thorough research will prepare you intellectually, at the lectern, it's imperative that you also look professional and in control—especially when there's a big sale riding on your performance. Even if there's a swarm of butterflies in your stomach, act calm and natural by imaging everyone in the audience is a good friend and rooting for you to win. Remember, the better you know your subject, the more relaxed you will feel. If you're thoroughly prepared, following these guidelines will help even the most timid speaker earn a standing ovation.

TIPS FOR GETTING PUMPED UP
BEFORE SHOW TIME

As you walk on stage to present your solution to prospective buyers, you want to be at your best, ready to knock their socks off. Here are a few tips for getting yourself prepped and pumped up before show time:

1. **Role-play:** For important presentations, do a couple of trial runs with your peers (and manager, if possible) to work out the kinks and hone your delivery.

2. **Compile a question list:** Think of all the possible questions customers might ask during and after the presentation, and then practice delivering your best answers.

3. **Arrive early:** Leave your office with plenty of time to spare, just in case you hit traffic or get lost. Avoid being late at all costs.

4. **Write the benefits:** Take out a blank piece of paper and write down from memory all the key benefits you plan to highlight in your presentation.

5. **Psych yourself up:** This is a great opportunity, and you're completely prepared. Remind yourself that the customer has already demonstrated confidence in you just by asking you to present.

6. **Keep the goal in mind:** You know what you want the customer to do at the end of your presentation—keep this at the forefront of your mind throughout the presentation.

10 TIPS FOR PRESENTATIONS

The following tips were provided by motivational speaker Steve Simms. Simms is president of Attitude-Lifter Enterprises and the author of Mindrobics: How to Be Happy for the Rest of Your Life.

1. **Consider the worst that can happen:** Your prospects aren't going to begin booing loudly and escort you bodily out of the building. Realistically, the worst-case scenario is that your audience will just sit there politely and not respond. So even the worst isn't that bad.

2. **Be an "inverse paranoid":** They believe that everyone is out to do them good! Realize that your audience wants you to do well.

3. **Instead, anticipate positive results and envision your presentation a success:** Fears are produced when we anticipate negative results.

4. **Focus on communicating the whole message instead of just saying the words correctly:** Use your notes or script as a road map, but keep in mind that you're trying to communicate ideas and sell yourself.

5. **Speak as though you're talking to one person:** Speak naturally, be sincere and passionate, and speak from your heart.

6. **Know your material:** Learn it so well that talking about it just comes naturally.

7. **Practice your presentations out loud in an empty room in front of a mirror:** Audiotape your presentations and listen to them.

8. **Look away from negative people who are manifesting negative body language:** Don't make eye contact with people who are sitting with their arms crossed and frowns on their faces. Make eye contact with the people who are smiling and nodding.

9. **Have fun with your presentations and let your personality come through:** Keep in mind that, in this busy world, it's an honor and privilege to have a group of people willing to listen to your ideas. When you get past the fear, presentations are fun.

10. **Presentation skills grow over time:** Don't be discouraged if your next presentation doesn't result in a sale. What's important is how well you communicate. You may not be elegant in your presentations, but if they produce results, you're a success. It means you're communicating and connecting with your audience.

FIVE TIPS FOR HANDLING Q&A SESSION LIKE A PRO

So you've finished your presentation and all went well. Now it's time to enter the unknown—the dreaded question-and-answer session. What if they ask you something you don't know? What if they challenge everything you say? What if they just won't stop asking questions?

Here comes international communications coach and speaker Diane DiResta to the rescue. In her book, *Knockout Presentations*, DiResta shows you how to handle the Q&A session with poise and polish. Here are five of her tips that actually might have you looking forward to your next Q&A session:

1. **Anticipate and prepare:** DiResta recommends making three lists. The first is a list of all the questions for which you know the answers. Write them down and remember the answers. The second is a list of questions for which you don't know the answers. Research the answers and write them down. On the final list write down the questions you dread. Plan a strategy for answering them in a nonconfrontational and nondefensive way.

2. **Listen:** "You need to listen, both physically and mentally, during Q&A," says DiResta. "Focus your energy and plant your feet. Listen to the person's entire message before you answer."

3. **Repeat or rephrase:** If you're presenting to a large group, it's important to remember that a question isn't yours—it belongs to the group, says DiResta. You don't need to repeat a question if you're in a small group or training session (unless it's a large group), or if it's a hostile question. If it's a hostile question, don't be defensive; just rephrase the question in a positive way.

4. **Answer concisely:** Keep your answers short and to the point.

5. **Move on to the next question:** To keep control of the meeting, DiResta suggests that you answer to the entire group but end your answer by speaking to someone other than the original questioner.

If you want the audience to know you are ready to close the meeting, DiResta suggests recapping your main points and leaving the listeners with an action to take or some food for thought.

PLEASE A CROWD: TIPS FOR EFFECTIVE GROUP PRESENTATIONS

When you present to a group of buyers, you want to captivate everyone's attention, excite them about your product or service, impress them with your in-depth knowledge, and compel them to give you the business. Following are veteran sales trainer Bob Frare's 11 critical tips for presenting to groups, adapted from his book *Partner Selling: A Dynamic Selling System for 21st Century*:

1. **Have a clear purpose:** At the conclusion of your presentation, what exactly do you want to accomplish? Do you want to inform, to entertain, to initiate a specific action, to train, what? Know this before you go in.

2. **Know what you're getting into:** How big is the room you'll be presenting in? How many people will be there? What's happening before you go on? What's happening after? Try to get in a little early to set the room up to your liking, so that you will be most comfortable.

3. **Cool as a cucumber:** Be yourself. Don't affect gestures or speaking tones that don't come naturally. Try to speak conversationally, and let the presentation flow out of you.

4. **Get a visual:** Visual aids make presentations much more interesting. For groups of less than 25, consider a flip chart. For large groups, you might use overheads, slides, or a multimedia display. A couple rules of thumb: Whatever

visual aids you use, don't stand in their way, and make sure people don't have to strain to see them.

5. **Live and learn:** Every public-speaking experience is an opportunity to learn and to develop your skills. Focus on the message and your confidence in what you're talking about, and that confidence will radiate and increase your comfort level.

6. **Salesperson, sell thyself:** If you can, do a little meet-and-greet before you present so that you become a real person, not just another presenter, to the meeting participants. If that's not possible, write your own introduction for whomever will be introducing you. That way you get to communicate precisely what you want to the group about you and your background.

7. **Hit the stage running:** Get that presentation going quickly, and keep a steady pace throughout. Poor presenters start slowly, and then the audience is lost for good. Grab their attention early and keep it with a crisp pace, solid eye contact, and a conversational tone.

8. **Make handouts available upon exit:** If you provide reading material during the presentation, you invite people to distraction. Don't compete with your own materials. Give participants written information to take with them when they leave.

9. **Be in good humor:** Before your presentation, try out any jokes or humorous observations you plan to use on colleagues or friends. The silence that follows a joke falling flat can kill your whole presentation. While humor can be great to add to a presentation, use it with caution.

10. **Wrap it up:** A good presentation always has a concise conclusion that leaves no doubt that the presentation is over. Find an effective way to accomplish this.

11. **Cue up the Q&A:** Figure out whether you want to answer questions during the presentation or afterwards, then let people know. If you'd like to get the Q&A session going, plant someone in the audience to ask an initial question. This will break the ice and make others more comfortable about raising their hands.

10 TIPS FOR VOICE IMPROVEMENT

By spending a few minutes a day working on the quality and tone of your voice, you can turn it into a personal and professional asset. Try these 10 tips toward improving your voice:

1. **Breathe normally—studied breathing is not the secret of a strong voice:** Taking in a deep breath wastes energy and can make you tense.

2. **Speak in the vocal range that is most natural and comfortable for you:** A vocal range can be extended, but only with training and over time.

3. **To control your pacing, speak in manageable groups of words:** Concentrate on one thought at a time and speak in shorter phrases, using fewer words per breath.

4. **Poor posture will throw off your air supply and your vocal support muscles:** Sit up straight especially when speaking over the phone.

5. **Keep mouth, throat, and jaw muscles relaxed:** This will avoid a nasal sound.

6. **Open your mouth and throat a little wider when speaking:** If they are too constricted, your sound can be cut in half.

7. **The vibrations generated by humming are great for revving up the voice:** Hum before picking up the phone.

8. **Excessive throat clearing is an irritant and can harm vocal cords:** It is better to swallow if your throat feels congested.

9. **Avoid dairy products for an hour or two before an important meeting, speech, or conversation:** Doing so will avoid stomach upset.

10. **Most fear of public speaking results from being inadequately prepared:** If you feel nervous, practice out loud, using your full voice for an important encounter or presentation.

By practicing these exercises, you can strengthen and change your voice. You'll never have to worry about sounding artificial or affected, and this will lead to more responsive customers.

CHAPTER 16

Using Selling Psychology

GIVING THE RIGHT SIGNALS

Sales professionals are forever searching for innovative and better ways to sell. But the excitement of your sales pitch or the impressive way you dress will matter little if you cannot sell yourself. How do you convey sincerity, exude confidence, and put others at ease? Body language, says communications expert Marjorie Brody.

The way you move speaks volumes. Visual signals can ruin your sales presentation even if you're unaware of your body's moves. Try to improve your sales numbers by working on facial expressions, eye contact, posture, and gestures. Here are some of Brody's tips for mastering the body's cues on your route to sales success.

1. **Posture:** Be controlled and comfortable. A relaxed image makes clients comfortable. Stand up straight and directly

face the other person. Raise your chin and hold arms relaxed at your sides, with hands open. Brody offers these posture prohibitions:

- Don't rock or sway when speaking.
- Don't pace.
- Don't cross your feet.
- Don't clasp hands in front of you.
- Don't put your hands on your hips.
- Don't join your hands behind your back.
- Don't cross your arms.
- Don't put hands in your pocket.
- Don't lean back in a chair.

2. **Gestures:** Head, arm, and hand movements reinforce what you want to convey, Brody points out. She says the best gestures spontaneously flow from your thoughts and feelings. During a presentation, vary your movements. Never use the same gestures repeatedly or risk drawing attention to the movement at the expense of the substance. Don't use a pointed finger. Never raise a fist.

3. **Eye contact:** By making eye contact, you're connecting with your listeners, according to Brody. That helps communicate your message. When presenting to a group, look directly at one person for several seconds, then move to the next face. With eye contact, nod sometimes to connect with the other person. However, don't overdo eye contact, Brody warns.

4. **Facial expressions:** For a week, watch your face in a mirror whenever you talk on the phone, Brody suggests.

Do you make any unfriendly or artificial expressions? You need to know if you're making strange faces in order to stop. The goal is to look pleasant and smiling in encounters with clients. Don't arch eyebrows, frown, or grimace. Practice and practice some more, advises Brody.

CRITICAL SALES PSYCHOLOGY SKILLS

1. **Never talk down to your customers:** Treat them as mature, intelligent adults, not as children who need you to lecture them.

2. **Show respect for your customer's values:** By showing you share their values, you create a strong bond.

3. **Empathize with your customer's feelings:** The best way to help customers is to accept and understand their feelings.

4. **Empower, don't overpower your customers:** Don't overpower with product knowledge. Instead, encourage your customers to ask questions. Know when to stop talking and start listening. Customer empowerment puts the customer in the driver's seat while the salesperson holds the road map.

5. **Maintain a professional attitude:** Professionals sell with integrity and treat people as equals regardless of gender, culture, color, speech, dress, or position within the company.

MIRROR, MIRROR (AND OTHER PERSUASIVE TIPS)

Effective selling starts with effective persuasion. Get your prospects to make the right decision with such tools as sales metaphors, behavioral pacing, and mental hinges. Find out how to use these and two other persuasion strategies by applying these tips from Dr. Donald Moine and John Herd:

1. **Mirror your buyer:** Prospects like to buy from people like them, so pacing, or mirroring key aspects of their character and actions, reveals that you two are birds of a feather. Observe you buyer's mood, speech rate, and volume, and opinions and beliefs. Without being a phony, let your own demeanor reflect your buyer's. When you disagree with buyers on an issue, focus on smaller aspects of it on which you can agree.

2. **Use humor and surprise:** You can lower your buyer's guard and open the door to a sale by cracking a simple joke or making a sensational statement to throw prospects off guard long enough to get them to open up to you.

3. **Read eye movements:** To understand how your buyers think, read their eye movements. When prospects look....

    -   ... up and to the left, they are thinking by remembering images. Sell with visual words—for instance, "Does this look clear to you?" or "Can I shed some more light on this feature?"

    -   ... up and to the right, they are thinking by creating new images. Again, sell with visual words.

- ■ ... down and to the left, they are thinking by talking to themselves. Use auditory words: "Does that sound good to you?" or "Should I amplify that point?"
- ■ ... down and to the right, they are using emotions and intuition. Sell with such feeling-action phrases as "step on it," "get a kick out of it," and "go out on a limb."

4. **Use sales metaphors:** Suggest pictorial relationships between objects or ideas. For example, Zero-Defect Program originator Phil Crosby illustrated the difference 1 percent can make by revealing that gorillas differ genetically from people by only 1 percent. With such vivid mental pictures, you can hold your buyer's attention and close more often.

5. **Get connected with mental hinges:** Tie persuasive suggestions to factual statements to sell your product. With such strong mental hinges as "make," "cause," "since," and "require," you can imply a necessary connection between one event and another: "Since you've told me your patients complain about Thorizide, Dr. Smith, you will be pleased to hear that our Vitazim causes side effects in fewer than 1 percent of patients."

CHAPTER 17

Win-Win Negotiations

EXPERT ADVICE FOR NEGOTIATING WITH PURCHASING MANAGERS

"If you are being chiseled down, you are in a negotiation," says Marilyn Nyman, president of Nyman Associates, a communications firm that provides coaching, consulting, and customized training. "Unfortunately, people are accustomed to viewing a negotiation as a win-or-lose situation. The better thing to do is to look at negotiation as building a relationship. At our company, we use a three-prong approach to doing that."

First, Nyman suggests that you choose a strategy before meeting with the purchasing manager. She recommends an interest-based strategy. "Go in with the idea that you are looking for common ground," she says. "What are their needs? What are their concerns? You also need to know what the purchasing manager's role is in that particular company. What kind of power does the purchasing manager have? Is the person just there to body-block and say no, which is sometimes the case, or can this person make his or her own decisions? Know your audience: Where do they fit in the organization? What pushes their buttons? Oftentimes they have more flexibility than they let on."

Nyman stresses that the relationship-building phase should not be overlooked. "People like to do business with people that they like," she says. "Use the art of the question. Ask a few open-ended questions to find out their needs. Let the other person talk so they can help you understand what they want. Remember, money is only one part of decision making," Nyman adds. "No purchasing decision is made just on dollars. See this as a process. Go in and build a relationship and then come back to negotiate."

The second part of the approach is dealing with emotion. "Most negotiations are driven by emotions," she says. "Manage your emotions and manage their emotions. How? Manage their emotions by reading their body language, listening to their tone of voice, and seeing everything they say as a concern that you have to address. If you go in with an idea of building a relationship instead of being uptight, you can focus on clients and read their emotions better."

The third and most important part of the approach is to help your client (in this case the purchasing manager) see your negotiation in terms of options and consequences. "If the purchasing manager says, 'We can only do it for this price,' don't say yes or no, say, 'Well, that's an option; the consequence may be that you won't get the kind of service that you want,'" Nyman advises. "Go in with three kinds of options; maybe one option is that if they pay less, they get less. Another option is that they can go with a competitor, but then they may find that the competitor doesn't have your track record. Option three is that you agree to the pricing and go ahead with the sale."

"The primary thing to remember is that you need to build a trusting relationship," says Nyman. "Sometimes that may mean that you don't get this particular sale, but remember, you will win in the long run."

FIVE TIPS FOR NEGOTIATING LIKE A PRO

In best-selling books like *What They Don't Teach You at Harvard Business School* and *The 110% Solution*, professional success guru Mark McCormack shared the lessons that helped build his reputation as one of the fiercest negotiating lions in the professional sports arena. Following are a few tips McCormack recommends to help sharpen your own negotiating claws:

1. **Don't get rankled:** Some people will open negotiations by criticizing you and your product, just to get you on the defensive from the start. Don't take it personally. Most likely, the attack is neither personal nor valid, so just weather the storm and move ahead as planned.

2. **Just say "no" to ultimatums:** Phrases like "Take it or leave it" and "You'll have to do better than that" sound like ultimatums, but they're more likely tactics intended to win concessions. Instead of conceding, treat the ultimatum as if it's the beginning, not the end of a negotiating process.

3. **Don't turn up the volume:** Buyers will often inquire about volume discounts, then try to get the same unit price

while nudging down the order size. Stick to your rate card until you win a guarantee of the volume purchase.

4. **Talk to the bad cop:** The good cop/bad cop negotiating tactic is designed to make you think you have an ally on the other side, softening you up for concessions. Instead, focus all your attention on winning over the bad cop, and you'll turn this tactic on its ear.

5. **Concede to win:** When you do make a concession, don't let on how much you're giving up. Take your time, drag out the concession, and imply that you're making a significant sacrifice, even if you're not. Then, when you grudgingly concede, ask the other side to sacrifice something greater in return.

NEGOTIATION TIPS FOR YOUR SALES CAREER

Most books on finding a new job focus almost exclusively on those tactics—improving your resume, making a good first impression, answering tough interview questions—that help you shine in the eyes of your future employers. No different is Dr. Pierre Mornell's book, *Games Companies Play: The Job Hunter's Guide to Playing Smart and Winning Big in the High-Stakes Hiring Game.* But what about after you've been offered the job? Mornell goes a bit further, providing tips on how to negotiate the best deal.

1. **Get to know 'em:** Establish a relationship with the person who will be negotiating with you. The better the

person knows you, the more willing he or she will be to put in the time to hammer out an agreement.

2. **Do your homework:** Gather information from comparable industries and positions. What are people in similar jobs being paid in the industry?

3. **Dream a little dream:** What is your pie-in-the-sky ideal in terms of salary, bonus, car allowance, vacation, health plan, and so on? Get to know ahead of time what your "dream" package is and you'll be better situated to judge what's eventually offered. Also, now's the time to mention any special things you need—weekends off for the army reserve, health coverage for a spouse's pre-existing condition, and so forth.

4. **Is there haggle room?** Your employers are probably reasonable people who will respond to your concerns and proposed solutions. Find out whether their offer is etched in stone or if they will listen to your thoughtful argument about why you need more.

5. **Who's over your shoulder?** If the company considered someone internally for the position that you won, that person could either prove to be a great ally or a potential antagonist. Talk to your new bosses about who these people are and what the company is prepared to do in case of a conflict. Consider ways to keep them happy, motivated, and productive.

6. **Keep your walkin' boots on:** Your trump card is always the willingness to walk away. But don't play that card idly. If you make the threat, you have to be ready to make good on it.

NEGOTIATE FOR A WIN-WIN

Here's a good question: What's a lot of fun—and vital to survival in a business climate in constant flux? Successful negotiation, says Ed Brodow, author of *Negotiate with Confidence*. Brodow, a former U.S. Marine and corporate sales executive, debunks the myth that negotiation is a game with winners and losers. "The anxiety we experience over the possibility of loss ranks negotiation right after a visit to the dentist," he writes. "Your anxiety will disappear when you recognize that both sides can have their needs met."

Here are some of Brodow's tips for negotiating:

1. **Everything is negotiable:** Once you're willing to challenge the other position's validity, then you can negotiate. Be assertive. Develop what Brodow calls "negotiation consciousness." Take nothing at face value. Make up your own mind. Ask for what you want.

2. **To make sure people hear you, listen:** Good negotiators probe with lots of open-ended questions and then listen well to the answers, Brodow explains. Learn how to listen and you'll easily quell many conflicts. Let others talk the most. Why? They'll tell you what you need to know.

3. **Do your homework:** Know other people's needs, their pressures, and their options.

4. **Be optimistic:** It's a proven strategy: If you aim higher and expect more, you'll do better and get more, according to Brodow. Salespeople should always ask for more than they anticipate getting.

5. **Mission: satisfaction:** Do what you can to help other people feel satisfied. That happens when their fundamental interests are fulfilled. Their basic interests are what they need, not what they say they want.

6. **Do this, get that:** Never give something away without getting something for it. Attach strings. No one-sided concessions allowed.

7. **Negotiate with options:** Always. You surrender the power to say no if you rely too heavily on the negotiation's success, Brodow says. Unfailingly, be willing to walk away.

NEGOTIATION TIPS FOR DEALING WITH A DEMANDING BUYER

1. **Don't sweat the small stuff:** Look to make concessions that only affect costs indirectly. By offering free training, extra services, extended warranty, free delivery, longer payment terms, and so on, you won't sacrifice price but will allow customers to think they are making a good deal.

2. **Play it cool:** Don't let your emotions get the better of you. This is true whether you're excited or upset by a development in the negotiation. Manipulative people look for emotional responses to know their tactics are working.

3. **Trading places:** Try to put yourself in the shoes of your opposite number. If the roles were reversed, what would you expect from the negotiation? What would you consider a reasonable request? Use this perspective to assess and evaluate your customers' demands.

4. **Check the record:** Talk to people who have negotiated with these people before. What are their tricks, strategies, and maneuvers? Now think of ways you can counter these tactics when they come up.

5. **Firm and fortune:** Don't be afraid to say no. But when you do, couch it in terms of your future relationship with customers. Show how your tenacity will work to the customers' advantage when they sign on with your company.

CHAPTER 18

Overcoming Objections

SELL THE BIG PICTURE

When famed television defense lawyer Perry Mason said, "Objection!" almost everyone in the courtroom knew that he was right and his challenge should be upheld. The same cannot be said when a customer raises objections during a presentation. A salesperson needs a reasoned response of a different sort to deal with a customer's hesitations and win the sale.

Common objections might seem to be the easiest to answer. Think again. With common objections, salespeople must always remember to give an uncommon response. And what is that? One that is carefully crafted to respond to the customer's individual underlying concerns.

Bob Arnold, a sales representative for Concord, New Hampshire-based CCR Data Systems, a point-of-sale (POS) system for restaurant operators, emphasizes the importance of knowing what is behind any objection in order to deal with the underlying issues. He is in a good position to do this because, having worked in the restaurant business for 35 years, he has seen it all before. "I can look them in the eye when they tell me that I don't know what it is like to be behind a line with dozens of orders from customers being thrown at me simultaneously and answer, 'Yes, I do.'"

What's one of the most common objections Arnold hears? Price. Restaurant owners always want to know what something is going to cost, so this is a constant objection waiting to happen. Arnold feels that people in the restaurant business share a strong "show-me" attitude. They want to know why they should invest thousands of dollars in his firm's Aloha POS system when they already have a system they feel works perfectly well. He has to show them, and prove to them, that his system will save them money. And he knows that the people he calls "serious owners" will listen.

"Serious owners are aware that the average bottom line will be between 0 percent and 5 percent, with many more at 0 than at 5. They understand that you should use a spatula to clean out that five-gallon mayonnaise jar before throwing it away—that saving pennies means saving dollars."

At the same time, this group of people keeps business records very private. Their reluctance to share information makes it hard for him to persuade them to build a return-on-investment model for the $15,000 or so they'll need to pay for his product.

Arnold is used to hearing "I'm not interested" from prospects when they hear the cost figure. Undaunted, Arnold digs deeper. "I need to learn more about their business by asking them questions," he explains, "and I help them learn more about mine."

First, Arnold breaks down the barriers. He asks a series of questions that allow customers to see the potential value of his product in several different scenarios common in the business. Arnold empathizes with customers. "OK, you probably aren't interested right now. But do you ever sit down with a pile of guest checks and find that dollars owed to you were not charged by your wait staff or were added incorrectly? Have you ever found guest checks in the trash and wondered whether they were honest mistakes or voids? Ever found that the little extra requests a waitperson gets were not charged to the customer? Ever have customers tell you that they order the same thing every week but are charged a different amount each time?

"I have experienced each and every one of these scenarios," Arnold explains. He knows what their answers will be, but he lets customers respond so that he can be specific about how CCR can help solve these problems.

Then he presents another feature he knows is important to this group: service and support on their terms. "A restaurant does not operate on a 9-to-5 schedule, and I tell them that they can talk with a live body when they need to. I can back it up by telling them that I was a customer of CCR for 35 years."

Quinn Brack, vice president of sales for RDI Marketing Services, a national B2B direct telephone-marketing firm based in Atlanta, says that when customers object they often are working on preconceived ideas about what salespeople are offering. He says common objections arise when customers do not see how his service fits their needs.

RDI provides a "niche service," he explains, that is usually part of a larger plan. The salesperson's job, consequently, is to get customers to focus on the part of the plan that the service will enhance. "You need to show them how what you are doing fits into their big picture. Focus on their individual needs."

Brack also knows the value of really understanding why customers think the way they do. He advises salespeople to listen carefully to each potential customer to know what they need. "You need to get on their level to understand what is behind their objections. I am always trying to get on their level and to clarify what they are saying.

"Our firm is selling a support solution. We are one piece of a marketing plan, and we need to show customers just how we fit in. To do that we have to have a good idea of their bid picture, their concept."

After 10 years in the B2B telemarketing business, Brack makes sure his sales representatives have considerable knowledge about their service to take to each new customer. Just knowing about a product or service, however, is not enough to overcome objections if customers don't see how the service fits what they're looking for. "It is important to make personal contact and focus on what each of those individuals needs," Brack urges. "In our business, objections are often based on obstacles the customer sees to achieving their goals with our service. I show customers how our niche service avoids the problems they anticipate."

Then, Brack notes, customers see salespeople not merely as sellers, but rather as valuable resources to help them build a marketing plan that will succeed on all levels.

IT'S A STALL WORLD: HOW TO GET YOUR CUSTOMERS TO MAKE A DECISION

"We need to find out what our budget is." "I need to speak with my partner first." "We haven't made up our minds yet whether we're going to move in that direction."

Even if you haven't heard these actual quotes in the past, you surely recognize them for what they are: classic stalls. Prospects stall for any number of reasons—insecurity about making a decision, fear of the unknown, lack of buying authority, the list goes on. Even more frustrating, they often provide phony excuses that mask the real reasons they won't make a decision today. According to one source, Peggy Madigan, a sales manager with Jacksonville, Florida-based WJXT-TV, all stalls boil down to one critical issue: The salesperson hasn't convinced the customer of the benefits.

To deal effectively with stalling customers—or better yet, to proactively eliminate the stall ahead of time—Madigan suggests the following strategies:

1. **Trust or bust:** "At the outset you have no idea what the customers' past experiences are or how they may feel about you and your company. Plus they're not going to come out and tell you what their hot buttons are, so you have to gain their trust before they'll open up about their insecurities."

2. **Objection overruled:** "With customers, you rarely get a second audience, so you have to make your first impression count. Get to know the customers' business and you can unearth potential objections early in the sales process and put them to rest."

3. **Bring your sizzle stick:** "Whatever you're selling, you're trying to get prospects to break out of business-as-usual and try something new. In our business it's advertising on TV. We play up the sexiness of television. What sizzle does your solution offer? Tap into that and you'll heat up the customers."

4. **Imagination is everything:** "One way to minimize discomfort is to have customers imagine what it would be like to use the product or to see the service in action. So if you feel like you're losing the customers, turn up the excitement a notch by having them consider the future possibilities with your product or service."

5. **Success breeds confidence:** "At its core a stall is about being unsure. One good way to deal with that insecurity is with success stories. We use stories that convey the positive power of television advertising, and they're useful in assuaging other prospects' doubts about us."

FIVE PERSUASIVE SELLING TACTICS PROVEN TO PREVENT OBJECTIONS

It's critical for any salesperson to know how to handle objections. Better than overcoming objections, however, is avoiding them altogether. Strong selling skills will help keep your prospects thinking about why they should buy your product instead of why they shouldn't. These five selling basics will help you sidestep the objections that stand between you and the sale.

1. **Sell value, not price:** What matters most for your customers isn't what they pay for your product, but what

they get for their money. Smart buyers appreciate a reasonable price, but if your product has the lowest price, they may suspect that it's not the highest quality. Point out to cost-conscious buyers that bargain hunting may help save money initially, but sacrifices in quality will cost more in the long run. Play up your product's versatility, reliability, and durability—all the things that make it well worth its price. Show sympathy for your prospects' budget concerns, but assure them that you want to sell them a product that they can rely on and that you can stand behind.

2. **Focus on benefits:** Experienced salespeople know that selling benefits is more effective than selling features, but it's also critical to sell the right features. Presenting benefits your prospects aren't particularly interested in probably won't move them to buy. One car buyer, for example, might be interested in a new sports car as a status symbol, whereas another may make a buying decision based on the car's speed and responsiveness. Analyze your target markets carefully and what your product can do for each. Ask your prospects open-ended questions and pay close attention to the comments they make for clues to help you pinpoint what will make them decide to buy.

3. **Put a price tag on benefits:** Your product's value will likely determine whether your prospect buys it. Once you know what your prospects want, find out what those benefits are worth to them. Will your product save time? Reduce labor costs? Increase profits? Remind your

prospects of all the things your product can do, the problems it can solve, and the goals it can help them meet. Compare the one-time price of your product to the amount of money your prospect will earn or save after years of using it. The clearer you make the distinction between what your prospects pay and what they get, the easier it will be for them to recognize your product's great value.

4. **Sell to people:** Even if you're certain that XYZ Company has a need for your product, don't forget that people make the buying decision. Ask yourself how your decision maker(s) will personally benefit from your product or service, then provide them with specific examples. If your product will reflect positively on your buyer by increasing production or reducing operating costs, for example, say so. Reassure your buyers that you have their best interests at heart, and provide testimonials from other buyers that show how buying your product was a wise decision for them. As you would with any prospect, find out what your decision maker's hot buttons are and push them.

5. **Appeal to emotion:** Although some people use logic to help them make buying decisions, we're all vulnerable to the power of our own emotions. Paint an emotional picture of your prospects using your product, including all the positive feelings they'll experience: "You'll be vey happy and excited when you see just what this software program can do for your salespeople. They'll be more efficient, and you won't have to worry about

making sure their contacts are organized or that they're using their time wisely. Isn't the peace of mind you'll enjoy well worth the price?" Describe the pride that comes from making a wise decision that creates a win/win situation for everyone.

Learning to overcome objections is a critical part of any salesperson's education—you have to know how to address any issues your prospect might raise. Observe some basic rules of persuasion, and you'll reduce the number of objections you hear. Give prospects all the right reasons to buy, and they'll give you fewer reasons not to.

FOUR QUICK TIPS FOR HANDLING OBJECTIONS

Ask questions to determine what issues besides price are of paramount concern to your customer. Sell to these concerns as a whole, to take the focus off price. Research your competition and your customers so you can perform a reality check on their claims.

1. **Silence can be golden:** Don't feel that you must immediately address each and every objection your customer raises.

2. **Help your customer sell the investment internally:** Assist in preparing return-on-investment (ROI) and total cost of ownership calculations to show how your product will help the bottom line.

3. **Look for other alternatives besides price:** Identify options that your customer may value, and offer these instead of a cost reduction.

4. **Never offer something for nothing:** Make sure you're getting something out of each and every concession you make.

HANDLING THE DREADED PRICE OBJECTION

It is a known fact that many customers learned their strategies for exacting price breaks from techniques developed during the Spanish Inquisition. And while there are many strategies for handling the price objection itself, author Tom Reilly suggests that by asking better probing questions during the qualifying stage, salespeople can frequently help avoid the dreaded price objection later on. Following are five of Reilly's tips for asking more effective questions, taken from his book *Crush Price Objections: Hold the Line On Prices.*

1. **Look long term:** Ask questions with long-term implications that force the customer to think about the future, not price. Sample questions include the following:
   - How long do you plan to use this product?
   - Where do you see your company five years from now?
   - How does this purchase relate to this project in the long term?

2. **Complicate matters:** Inquire about more complex, broad-based issues that might supersede price concerns. Sample questions include:

   - What is your definition of value?
   - What are the three greatest defining trends in your industry?
   - What are the most frequent drains on your profitability?

3. **Play to your strengths:** Ask questions that highlight the value you bring to the customer. Sample questions might include the following:

   - How important is a rapid turnaround time?
   - What benefits would you gain from outsourcing your training?
   - What's your greatest concern surrounding quality?

4. **Go negative (sort of):** Use questions to bring attention to possible deficiencies in the service the customer may currently be experiencing. Ask

   - What do you like or dislike about your current product?
   - How will your current product handle your needs 18 months from now?
   - How is your delivery?

5. **Sneak price in:** To determine how much of a price battle you'll face, ask questions that indirectly broach the topic. Sample questions include these:

   - What is your decision process like?
   - What budget range are you working with?
   - What is most important to you in a potential solution?

CHAPTER 19

Closing Every Time

TO CLOSE ... TRY THE PORCUPINE TECHNIQUE

Technically, it's known as a minor close, or trial close, but it's one of the most effective and most immediately usable of all. The "Porcupine Technique" deserves to be better known, for it will work for you in many ways. Use the Porcupine to generate an agreement going into the final "tie-up." It leads nicely and naturally into pay dirt. The Porcupine is a way to answer a question with a question of your own, in a way that helps you maintain control of the interview. At the same time you find out what's on the prospect's mind:

PROSPECT: Does it come in light green?

YOU: Would you like it in light green?

PROSPECT: Yes, I would.

YOU: I can have it already for you next week.

Here's how this technique got named: If someone tossed you a porcupine, what would you do? You'd toss it right back. When you do this, usually you find yourself in a more favorable position.

Many times in selling you'll get a question that can be answered only with a "yes" or a "no," and often this puts a brake on conversation. Or, you might be asked to give information that's important to the prospect, and you have nothing to say. However, if you throw the porcupine back, you can take command:

PROSPECT: Could I take delivery by the first of the month?

YOU: Does taking delivery by the first best suit your needs?

PROSPECT: Yes, that's the best time.

YOU: I'll see that it's done!

Years ago, sales experts determined that any question you ask the prospect must cause conversation and participation or it has little sales value. Veteran lecturer and sales trainer Fred Herman cautioned, "Never tell them anything you can ask them." The Porcupine response can give you valuable information on which to base the remainder of your presentation:

PROSPECT: Is this applicable for computer programming?

YOU: Would you like to have it programmable?

PROSPECT: No! I think I could handle it better in the general ledger.

YOU: Then I think you're going to enjoy working with this system. It's entirely applicable to the general ledger.

If the salesperson had gone on selling computerization, he would have sold himself down the river. Instead, one simple return question and, without dictating to the prospect, the salesperson found out one key point of information. The prospect was not being lectured, but rather "had a hand in things." By taking a part in the conversation and getting his opinions known, the prospect felt more satisfied with the whole procedure.

Following are other examples of effective uses of the Porcupine method:

PROSPECT: Will this policy feature a cash value?

YOU: Is a cash value important to you?

PROSPECT: Definitely not! I don't want to be paying extra for cash value.

YOU: I'm happy to hear you say that. Let me show you how our 10-year term policy works ...

PROSPECT: Can you put this sort of shrubbery in direct sunlight?

YOU: Do you have a sunny spot in mind?

PROSPECT: Yes, I was thinking of the side of the house.

YOU: Right! It will look nice out there.

Another advantage of the Porcupine is that it helps the salesperson gain control of the presentation. Often, by asking an unexpected question, a prospect may catch you off guard. The Porcupine Technique helps you collect your thoughts during the brief time you are waiting for the prospect's answer to your question. When this answer comes, you have gained the initiative and are back with your thoughts in gear—ready to retain control of the interview and carry it through to the close.

CLOSING TIPS

Following are a few out-of-the-ordinary strategies you can use to persuade customers to put pen to paper:

1. Looking for one phrase to reassure customers that you will always do right by them? Try this: "I will spend your money as if it were my own."

2. As you close, hold up a $50 bill, tear it in half and give one half to the customer. Then hold up the remaining half and say, "If you can find a better value for your money, I'll give you the other half."

3. Put it in writing. Print up a list of services you can personally guarantee to the customer: "I will return all phone calls the same business day," "I will always treat your time as a precious commodity," for example. Offer this sheet to the customer in exchange for the business.

CLINCH THE CLOSE WITH BETTER QUESTIONS

The following tips were provided by Ron Karr of Karr Associates Inc.

Successful closing depends not on what you say at the end of a sales call, but on how you conduct it up to that point. On your next call, take these three steps to question more effectively and get the answers you need to close:

1. **Don't let no throw you:** After you hear a no, simply find out what the buyer thinks your offer lacks. Include a value proposition—a formal recommendation that satisfies buyers' wants and needs while providing the impetus for them to accept the offer. Good value propositions always offer buyers greater profitability, improved productivity, reduced costs, or a competitive edge.

2. **Ask issue-based questions that address the four benefit areas of the value proposition to clarify what's missing from your proposal, and encourage buyers to offer specific information about each challenge** For example, if a prospect is reviewing retirement options, you might say, "Mrs. Smith, what are the three most important things you want your investments to achieve for you?"

3. **Ask clarification and consequence questions.** By asking buyers to clarify what quality means to them or how they define "a good deal," you can better understand how to meet their needs. Consequence questions point to a solution's perceived value and highlight the outcomes buyers face if they do not act. Remember:

   Perceived Value = the Cost of No Change
   — the Cost of Change.

HOW TO CLOSE A SALE WITHOUT CAUSING PROSPECT PANIC

Prospects expect the salesperson to close the sale, yet when the salesperson does ask for the order, the prospect often panics, stalls, or argues. When a salesperson makes the prospect panicky by asking for the order too early or inappropriately, the entire selling effort may ride off into the sunset.

The following five types of closes will help you close without causing prospect panic.

1. **The assumptive close:** The assumptive close assumes the customer is going to buy. You have used your questioning skills and objection-handling techniques to provide your customer with the information needed to make an informed buying decision. You have received agreement along the way that your proposal is a winning solution to his or her problem. All you need to know now are things like delivery, installation, financing, and purchase order information.

2. **The action close:** The action close requires the prospect to do something. You have made your presentation and received the necessary agreement. Now you are ready to get the final agreement, the order. You might ask that your prospect take some action that will begin the order process. This includes completing the purchase order, or determining the number of work stations to begin with.

   The action close is effective with those prospects who exhibit an "active personality" style. They are the people who always need to do something before it becomes official. They feel more comfortable when they get physically involved.

3. **Minor-point close:** This closing techique asks for an "insignificant" decision where a "yes" answer implies the prospect has bought. Normally this type of close is

made many times during a sales presentation to gain the prospect's agreement along the way. Each time you present a feature that provides the prospect with a needed benefit, ask for his or her agreement. Once you have amassed a series of these agreements, it is logical to ask for the order.

Minor-point closes are effective with people who like to follow a step-by-step approach. They are the prospects who talk in terms of, "First, we need ... second, we have to ... and third, we'll want to ...."

4. **Alternate-choice close:** The alternate-choice close provides your prospect with two or three positive choices, instead of choosing between yes or no. Both answers result in getting the order. The only difference is a small detail that does not affect the decision to buy.

    The alternate-choice close is effective with those prospects who like to make decisions. It must be used at the right time. This is usually after the presentation has been made and all the questions and concerns are answered.

5. **Invisible close:** This is a favorite because it is very conversational and avoids "decision panic" for your prospect. The invisible close uses a series of action closes and minor point closes that indicate your prospect has bought. The invisible close gently takes your prospect through a series of questions that need to be answered. It is effective with those prospects who need to be helped along with their decisions.

No matter which close you use, always start by reviewing the important benefits to your prospect. Paraphrase the key points of your solution and ask if the prospect agrees with you. Then choose a plan that requires the involvement (buy-in) of your prospect. This makes the prospect feel like a part of the solution and will make selling much easier!

GETTING PAST YES

Sales training almost always focuses on all the steps that go into getting to "yes." But for the sales professional interested in long-term business and repeat customers, what happens after "yes" may be just as important as everything that led to the buying decision. Following are some tips from Thomas J. Leonard, author of *Working Wisdom*, for keeping your customers happy after all the contracts are signed.

1. **Congratulations in order:** Of course you're happy for yourself, but what about your customers? Focus on why this is a great deal for them and it will reinforce the messages you expressed during the sales process.

2. **Look forward:** Offer a suggestion about the product's performance that reinforces the buying decision. Say something like, "With this program in place I think you'll find XYZ becomes much easier for you."

3. **What gives?** Now's a good time to find out what motivated the buying decision. Say, "May I ask why you chose this model today?" The answer will help you position future clients as well.

4. **Open up the floor:** Your previous questions were focused on determining needs. Now you should offer to answer

any questions customers have about being customers rather than prospects.

5. **Plot a course:** Let customers know where the relationship moves from here on and how you will continue to work for them. Say, "Now that this is settled, here are the three things I will do for you in the next week...."

6. **Call waiting:** Get their OK for you to call within 30 days. This will let them know you will continue to service them, and it also gives you a great opportunity to troll for referrals.

7. **Out with doubt:** Take a moment to ferret out any lingering doubts about the sale. This will solidify your reputation in the customers' eyes as a problem solver and a caring sales professional. Ask, "Do you have any remaining doubts about the purchase that I can help you with?"

CHAPTER 20

Upselling Techniques

UPSELLING REQUIRES KNOWING THE CUSTOMER'S NEEDS AND BEING PREPARED TO OFFER OPTIONS

It takes a lot of time and money to develop and keep an account. Once you have it in the bag, it makes sense to sell as much to that account as you possibly can. By carefully upselling products and services that your customers really need and will value, you could double, triple, or even quadruple your business in a year. While upselling can be a powerful sales tool, you must follow a few simple rules to make it work.

What are the secrets of the upsell? Mike Weber, sales manager at Young Electric Sign Company of Las Vegas, Nevada, and Sadler Evans, account executive for Comcast Cable Advertising of Huntsville, Alabama, share their thoughts about what works in the world of upselling.

"Upselling is largely a matter of selling your company and pushing the quality factors of your product and customer image," says Weber. "Before you can upsell, you need to develop a relationship with the prospect. We bring prospects into our facility and show them our manpower, what we're capable of doing, and the quality of our work. We want them to be assured their sign is going to be a piece of jewelry. And if they need support, we do it from A to Z with such services as one-stop shopping and on-time delivery."

Weber feels the cornerstone of selling—especially when trying to upsell a client—relies on continuously qualifying the prospect throughout the buying process.

"Qualify, qualify, qualify, and then qualify some more," advises Weber. "As the prospects get closer to making the purchasing decision, their wants and needs are going to change, and salespeople have to recognize and keep on top of those changing needs."

Weber also emphasizes the importance of image, or perceived image, on the part of the customer. "It's a question of how much money a customer has to spend and what kind of image the business wants to project," he says. "It's like buying a suit. If a guy is comparing a $595 suit with a $1,200 Armani, the question in his mind is whether it's worth spending another $600 to look like a million bucks. And if he looks like a million bucks in the more expensive suit, then which tie is he more likely to buy—one that costs $50 or one that costs $90?

"We do a lot of upselling in the design phase of our transaction," Weber points out. "We show a customer a rough of the desired sign and then show a rendition of something better. It's a matter of image. Regardless of budget restrictions, the client really wants a Cadillac and not something cheesy. It's a process to get the client to see the value of the $50,000 sign, even though the original budget was for $35,000. We explain the benefits of spending the additional $15,000 to project a better image.

"For example, if a customer wants to buy a set of neon letters for $35,000, our designers will show what it would look like with a ring of white around the letters, and it really pops the impression. It's an automatic $10,000 upsell, and we feel they are dollars well spent. It's ultimately the customer's choice and we don't want to oversell, but we are committed to giving options," concludes Weber.

While cable advertising and electric display signs are two different products, Evans agrees with Weber on the importance of ongoing qualifying and selling to the real needs of the prospect.

"When I first started in sales it took me a while to realize how to upsell a client," says Evans. "I didn't have enough business in my funnel and was taking too little money from too many people, so I decided to start selling quality advertising schedules.

"Qualifying isn't a one-time, static thing," Evans explains. "Needs change as companies reach objectives, and you need to stay on top of where your customer's business is going and how you can be an honest part of the solution."

Evans notes that salespeople are sometimes to desperate to hit their monthly sales goals they forget their role of consultant to their customers. "When I started putting together a higher-quality product, my customers started seeing results," says Evans. "I became more of a consultant instead of just a salesperson scrambling to make his monthly numbers. My clients recognized that and knew I could be trusted to sell them what they needed."

Evans points out that being a consultative salesperson means being completely honest with the customers, even if it means losing a sale in the short term. "It's tough when a customer has $50 per week to spend. I explain it's better holding on to that money until there is enough to buy a schedule that's going to work and do more good," says Evans.

"I try to upsell clients to the point where I think the advertising schedule will work," explains Evans. "I have one client who wanted to start out at $600 per month and I thought that at least $750 was needed for effective advertising. The customer went for the higher buy. It worked, and now that company is a really solid account, spending around $2,300 per month.

"Sometimes upselling and creating greater value for a customer doesn't have to do with up-front costs, but instead deals with customer concerns and fears," Evans points out. "For example, we produce commercials for our clients, and the cost can range from $250 and up per spot. We had an attorney who was really hesitant about local cable advertising and concerned about getting lost in the clutter with mediocre commercials. We took the time to address all his production concerns and produced two spots for him, and now he's spending $5,000 a month. But we wouldn't have gotten to that point if we didn't add value and upsell the package by addressing and eliminating the concern about production quality.

"The only way you can succeed in upselling is to believe 100 percent in what you're doing, think ahead, service your clients, and create relationships that are sincere," says Evans.

"If you're constantly worried about making your quota, don't even bother to try."

PREPLANNING GUIDE: IDENTIFY UPSELLING OPPORTUNITIES

If you're not used to approaching existing customers with upselling in mind, prepare yourself before walking into your next meeting by asking yourself the following:

1. Based on my ongoing research, how can I direct the conversation to highlight new challenges, shifting strategic approaches, and changing market realities where my product or service can make a difference?

2. What specific solutions have I identified that offer the greatest upselling opportunities with this account?

3. How can I leverage the positive results other customers have experienced by making similar additional purchases?

4. When during the conversation should I mention additional solutions that may be of interest?

5. What, precisely, am I going to say to segue into the upselling conversation (e.g., "Our XR-450 model has worked so well for you, I thought I should let you know about another breakthrough design we've developed...")?

SEVEN KEY SKILL FOR SUCCESSFUL UPSELLING

1. **Continuously qualify your prospect:** Learn what the customer's objectives and needs are at different levels. Once financial stakes increase, needs may change.

2. **Become a product and marketing expert:** The more you upsell, the more you're expected to justify increased client spending. Show your client why moving up a level will increase revenue, provide a better image, be more efficient, and so on.

3. **Start selling on a higher product level or price point:** Customers very seldom move more than two price points, so don't always start with the lowest-price product or service.

4. **Have options ready:** Subscribe to the Sears "good, better, best" theory, and have alternate selections or programs available.

5. **Be aware of ancillary product sales opportunities:** Your job as a professional salesperson is to sell the customer everything needed to enjoy or be satisfied with the purchase.

6. **If you don't feel the level of purchase is high enough to satisfy the anticipated needs or objectives of the customer, say so:** It may mean a postponed sale, but you build credibility and trust.

7. **Remember: People buy by emotion and justify by logic:** What a customer thinks is needed or wanted during the first meeting with you may not really be what is required. Ask probing questions, and listen and watch for signals that give away real customer needs.

CHAPTER 21

Follow-up for Better Sales

WIN SALES WITH FOLLOW-UP

James Feldman, motivational consultant, facilitator, and speaker, has a secret weapon in his marketing arsenal. What's the often overlooked, simple tool that many businesses forget to use? Follow-up. With existing customers or potential clients, follow-up marketing can ring up thousands of dollars in annual sales and profits. Here's how Feldman suggests using this marketing method to your benefit.

Follow Up with Current Customers

Consider advertising and marketing expenses. Even if it costs nothing to place an ad for a product or service in some media, look at the price of the time it takes to write and place the ad.

"It costs every business quite a bit of money to create a sale and a customer." When you add a new product to a line, advertising and marketing expenses can rise. How can you cut costs instead? Follow up with current customers and you may lower marketing costs and boost the chances of repeat sales. Everyone shops at favorite spots, returning again and again because they can count on good treatment, products, or service. So remember to send a mailing to established customers. "Simple, effective, and powerful follow-up with your customers will produce results," Feldman says.

Follow Up with Potential Customers

Every day customers tell Feldman they became clients because of his follow-up. Deluged by offers, clients report that many businesses just e-mail information and then disappear, never to be heard from again. As a well-planned marketing technique, follow-up often gets a warm reception from prospects. "It shows that you are concerned about your business and want to create happy customers instead of looking for the quick buck."

But beware. Develop a follow-up process that never makes prospects feel they're being harassed or pushed into a decision. Consider some of Feldman's tips for follow-up with potential customers:

- Decide how many times and how often to follow up with a given prospect. It depends on pricing and the difficulty of explaining a product or service. Here's a rule of thumb: The greater a product's price and complexity, the more times you will need to follow up. Your goal is to have prospects remember you and have time to consider the offer.

- Establish a tracking system. It should track follow-up with each prospect.

- Develop follow-up letters carefully. What should letters say? Make sure prospects understand the product and offer so they can make an informed decision. Use facts and avoid hype. Add bonuses or special offers when possible. Refresh their memory of your product or service.

  In your final follow-up letter, thank prospects for considering what you sell. Tell them it's your last letter. If you don't get a response, remove them from your files.

- Honor prospects' requests. Do they want more information? Provide it. Do they want to be removed from your files? Do it. If you don't, you'll get a bad reputation. "A happy customer tells three [others] and a mad customer tells 10, and on the Internet you might even multiply that by thousands," Feldman cautions.

"Marketing is selling what the customer wants . . . not what the factory makes," Feldman says. When customers initially get in touch, they want to reach a goal or find a particular solution. Focus on that target and you'll hit it.

THE IDEAL FOLLOW-UP PLAN

"Doing a great job of marketing your company actually could hurt you if you have poor follow-up procedures," says Kathy Ellis, marketing coach and owner of The Business Lab. "Nothing can ruin a great marketing plan faster than failure to follow up on the leads generated by your plan. Having a game plan on how to follow up can help solve this problem." Ellis outlines her suggested game plan.

Determine the Ideal Way to Follow Up

"With your team, create in-motion scenarios. These are scenarios that depict the process from the time your clients or prospects discover that what you offer can help them to the time they go in-motion and respond to you in some way—by telephone call, e-mail, reply card or walk-in," says Ellis. Next, imagine, role-play, or write out these scenarios. This will help you prepare for them. Here are some questions to answer during the scenario process:

- How does the conversation sound?
- What is the tone?
- What message is conveyed?
- Who are your prospects or clients?
- What do they need?
- Why do they need it?
- What actions are necessary?
- When will you meet them?
- What will you send?
- How might they respond?

Create a System

Next, says Ellis, create a checklist or outline of the actual steps involved. Ellis provides the following scenario: Assume that as a result of reading your newsletter, a prospect requests your free services booklet via e-mail. The follow-up steps might go something like this:

1. Respond to e-mail within 24 hours.

2. In your response thank the prospect and include any general or prewritten response.

3. Research the prospect by visiting his or her Web site.

4. Send out the services booklet with a cover letter addressing the prospect's specific business or industry.

5. Send the package via Priority Mail within 24 hours of receiving e-mail.

6. Make tickler follow-up call within three to five business days of the package leaving the office.

7. Call the prospect on a determined day. Verify that the package has been received, answer questions, and determine next steps.

After you've completed the above steps, it's equally important that you schedule an appointment and a follow-up call, send any necessary information, and decide on a follow-up date. Put all these dates on your calendar. Keep a log listing prospect's name, company, date contacted, and what marketing effort the prospect responded to.

"While these tracking and follow-up activities are time-consuming, a consistent program of tracking your marketing efforts is integral to knowing where you stand when you put forth the effort to market to clients or prospects," says Ellis. "This goes back to the essence of congruency and consistency and how they impact trust. If, because of some marketing effort on your part, a prospect contacts your company but you fail to follow up, then that prospect will immediately discount any further marketing effort on your part."

FOLLOW UP, UP, AND AWAY

Sales literature extols its value, sales trainers preach its virtues, and sales managers exhort their sales reps to do it, yet effective follow-up remains among the least utilized weapons in the sales professional's arsenal. Why? Because it's time-consuming, frequently uninteresting, and typically only bears fruit in the far-distant future. But according to Gary Volentine, a marketing manager with automobile replacement parts manufacturer Federal Mogul, follow-up is an area where a sales organization can genuinely shine and put distance between itself and the competition. Volentine identifies five specific reasons why salespeople should follow up diligently.

1. **Brush fires, not conflagrations:** "I'm the funnel between the customer and my company's internal departments. When you follow up with customers and find out proactively about their issues, you make sure the little issues don't escalate and become big problems."

2. **The best teacher:** "Once you've followed up with a customer to make sure everything worked out, you then gain invaluable experience that you can pass on the next person who faces a similar problem. Plus, you know everything was resolved. And if you disseminate your experience to the rest of your company, you can help others who may also be dealing with that issue."

3. **Trust builder:** "Most people don't do a very good job following up. When I do follow up with customers, I hear such comments as 'This is unusual' or 'People don't usually call to find out whether everything actually worked out.' They appreciate it, and it builds a level of trust so that they're more willing to share other concerns and issues that may arise."

4. **A two-way street:** "Follow-up also goes in the other direction—not only with the customer but also internally. While your allegiance always lies with your company, you're also the customer's advocate within your organization. So you have to be persistent and follow up with other departments in your company to make sure the customer is getting the best possible service. My colleagues all have several things on their plates, and if I'm not diligent, they might not place the priority on my request and it might not get done in a timely manner."

5. **In the fore:** "Follow-up just keeps you in the forefront of the customer's mind. When you're quick to respond and the customer knows you'll generate creative solutions that resolve their problems, they'll be more receptive to take your calls, strengthening the lines of communication. If you don't address the customers' concerns, they will be hesitant to talk to you and the relationship will founder."

EIGHT AGGRESSIVE FOLLOW-UP STRATEGIES THAT TURN HOT PROSPECTS INTO BIG PROFITS

1. **Qualify leads carefully:** Make sure your leads are qualified to do business with you. Each one should meet your

criteria in at least four areas: wants/needs, financial resources, decision-making authority, and time frame. Design a system to identify promising leads and give them top priority. Requalify your leads occasionally to make sure you're giving the most follow-up time to your most promising prospects.

2. **Focus on setting the appointment:** Instead of trying to sell on your first or second call to a prospect, just try to get an audience with him or her. Design a benefit statement that will convince the customer to grant you an appointment. Keep calls brief to show respect for your prospect's time. Take responsibility for all callbacks and contacts and—remember—ask for what you want.

3. **Vary your contact:** A call, package, or fax will have more impact if it's reinforced with another form of contact. Follow phone calls with a letter or fax outlining the highlights of your conversation and confirming any action steps your prospect approved. Call your prospects within a week after you send a letter or package to confirm receipt, personalize your contact, and show your customers that you're persistent in your desire to help them.

4. **Take advantage of the fax:** Chances are your prospects can screen your calls, and many receive so many it may be difficult for your information to grab your prospects' attention. They may attach a greater sense of urgency to a fax, however. If your prospects spend 10 more seconds reading your material because you faxed it, that may be all the time you need to pique their interest. Be sure to

personalize your faxes—make them brief and simple, featuring clear benefit statements.

5. **Establish a follow-up schedule:** Remember that last month's "no" may be this month's "yes." Try to touch base with prospects regularly without being intrusive. Also, group prospects according to when you expect them to buy (within 30 days, within 60 days, etc.). The sooner you expect a prospect to buy, the more frequently you should stay in touch. Design a follow-up contact schedule like the one shown on page 181 to help you keep track of your prospects and the contacts you make with them.

6. **Collect leads on follow-up calls to established customers:** Repeat customers need to know they aren't being taken for granted, so contact them regularly to make sure you're still meeting their needs and expectations. If you've provided good service to these customers, don't hesitate to ask for the names of friends or associates who might benefit from your product or service.

7. **Send literature sparingly:** If prospects are interested in your product or service, you can withhold literature and make additional contacts to provide more information and build rapport. Withholding literature also keeps your product information customized for each individual prospect. Use your customers' requests for information to gauge their level of interest in your product.

8. **Make every contact count:** Whether you phone, fax, or mail, make each contact professional and engaging. Write clear, concise business letters and include a benefit or promotional item to sustain the prospect's interest

in each one. Plan your contacts before you call, and try to add value to the call—even if it's just some new information related to their industry or business.

To many prospects, contacts-initiating sales calls are a dime a dozen. Outstanding salespeople, however, can prove themselves and win a customer by pursuing prospects thoughtfully and persistently. By carefully analyzing your current follow-up system and its effect on your prospects, you can make improvements that will encourage prospects to follow up on your efforts—with a sale.

CHAPTER 22

Time Management Skills

EFFECTIVE TIME MANAGEMENT

The following advice is from Tom Reilly, president of Sales Motivational Services, a firm that specializes in sales and sales management training.

If the average salesperson were to become a half hour more time-effective during the day, this would mean an average additional $4,800 in personal income annually.

One cannot be totally effective in sales unless time is used as an ally rather than an adversary. Effective salespeople understand time and its three contingencies. First, good time management is good self-management. One does not manage time; rather, we manage ourselves within the constraints of time. Second, good time management is substituting one habit for another. We currently do things either efficiently or inefficiently. Time management is then a function of substituting effective habits for ineffective ones.

The third time management contingency is that these habits must be consistently applied. They must become part of our everyday life. You do not practice time management one day and not the next. One day's good habits do not bring lasting results. It is no different than fueling your car or body. One tank of gas only takes you so far. One meal does not last forever. Time management must be practiced daily to enjoy any substantial benefits.

The Time Log

There are three things that effective salespeople do to better manage themselves and, hence, their time. First, they perform an analysis of their current practices. This is called a time log. Before one can suggest ways to improve, it is necessary to determine how time is being misused. This way, adjustments in habits are based on insight rather than guesswork.

Here are some suggestions for the log. Use a three-week time span. This will balance any atypical days. Begin from the time you leave the house in the morning and conclude when you arrive home in the evening. Develop different categories for activities like travel, waiting, administrative work, and so on. When you have completed your log, ask two questions in your analysis: "What would happen if I eliminated this activity?" and "Who else could do this for me?" Time logs require self-discipline. Once you have done this for a few days, it becomes a habit and is no longer perceived as an inconvenience. In fact, many people report that they enjoy doing it so they can see where their time is being used or misused.

Multiply Yourself

The second thing that effective salespeople do to become better self-managers is that they actively seek ways to multiply themselves. Effective salespeople use the post office to their advantage. They personally invest in direct-mail pieces. They send literature, form letters, thank-you notes, journal articles, newsletters, or anything else that will keep their names in front of the customer.

Effective salespeople also multiply themselves by seeking ways to use the telephone. Follow-up, arranging for appointments, pre-call qualifying, and canvassing are just a few of the ways that effective salespeople will multiply themselves with the phone.

Referral selling and enlisting the aid of other people are other valuable ways to multiply yourself. The principle is simple: Get others to do some of your work for you! Referral selling is very effective because the customer qualifies the prospect for you.

The single most effective way to multiply your efforts is by developing the mind-set that trading one's money for more time is a bargain at any price. Always be willing to invest money to gain time. Money is a replaceable commodity; time is not!

Planning Power

The third thing effective salespeople do to become better self-managers is that they plan. If it sounds simple, it is!

The effective salesperson begins planning by outlining his or her goals or aspirations. Once the objectives are established, a strategy is then developed to achieve them. The effective salesperson couples dogged persistence with a clear vision of the goal to achieve more. The ineffective salesperson loses sight of the goal because he or she has become too immersed in the mechanics of achieving the goal. This is demonstrated by salespeople who are more concerned with the number of sales calls they make than the number of sales they make. It is their obsession with activity versus results that causes their ineffectiveness.

SMART STRATEGIES FOR MANAGING TIME EFFECTIVELY

There are enough hours in the day—just master your schedule to eliminate the time drains that suck the efficiency out of your life. Following are a few tips from Jan Jasper, author of *Take Back Your Time: How to Regain Control of Work, Information, and Technology.*

1. **Purge the guilt:** Accept the fact that you can't do it all. Your life is the sum total of your decisions—don't feel guilty if you have to eliminate some things.

2. **Work your schedule backward:** Instead of writing down all the tasks you need to accomplish today and then passing the weeks, months, and years that way, begin at the end. What do you need to accomplish this month? With that goal in mind, create your plan for today, tomorrow, and so on.

3. **Stop waiting:** Carry reading material or a pen and paper with you everywhere you go. Turn wasted time spent waiting for others or in line into useful time.

4. **Quit the gild:** The minutiae of the day's tasks don't have to be done perfectly. Instead of endlessly polishing that letter or making sure your house is spotless, take that time for something that is more pressing and which will move you closer to your goals.

5. **Late ain't great:** Consider eliminating chronic late-comers from your client list. Would the time you spend waiting be better spent seeking out new opportunities?

6. **Caught in the Web:** When you're on the Internet, always ask, "Am I pursuing a specific goal or am I needlessly surfing?"

7. **Take notes:** Keep a selection of thank-you notes on hand so that you can use waiting time to write personal notes to customers and prospects.

TIME MANAGEMENT TIPS

1. **Why are you wasting time?** For many salespeople, ineffective time management is not about disorganization—it's about the fear of rejection. If you're doing everything but making calls, address your fear of rejection head-on and the time management problem will become much less of an issue.

2. **Always ask, "Is this the best use of my time?"** Remember, 20 percent of your activities deliver 80 percent of your revenues, so operate as much in that 20 percent sphere as possible.

3. **Get more face time:** Time spent with customers is the only time that makes sales. Take a stopwatch and record how much time you spend during the week with customers. The next week, try to increase that figure by 10 percent. Then keep upping the ante each successive week.

4. **Prioritize:** Being each day with the highest-value task on your to-do list, even if it's the most unpalatable, and stick with it until it's done. Then move on to the second, third, and so forth.

SEVEN THIEVES OF TIME ... THAT CAN STEAL YOUR SALES AWAY

When did you last compute what even one hour of your selling time is worth? Traveling to prospects, waiting for customers, piles of paperwork—all necessary activities that eat away at your productive day. If you want to minimize time lost and maximize the time you have for selling, read the following suggestions:

1. **Thief #1—Travel:** Two calls on customers that are three hours traveling time apart consume as much time as six calls on customers that are closer to one another. Simple arithmetic, maybe, but many salespeople don't realize

that traveling time takes away valuable selling time. To get more sales mileage out of your wheel spinning, plan each day to spend a minimum amount of time on travel between calls. If your territory is in the city, spend the day in the same neighborhood or suburb. If your territory covers the countryside, spend the day in neighboring towns. When you must meet with two very important customers whose offices are far apart, and you are taking a plane or the subway, use the time to catch up on your paperwork or reading. If you are driving, use the travel time to listen to sales and motivational tapes. This way, you'll arrive at your sales call ready to sell.

2. **Thief #2—Unpreparedness:** The salesperson who knows little about the product or customer will take the longest to make a presentation. The salesperson who is most thoroughly prepared will always need the shortest time to present the product and its benefits. Since compressing an idea into a brief but adequate presentation can be far more successful for you than floundering around for an hour or more, prepare your presentations. Know what you are going to say. Don't waste your own and your prospect's time searching for just the right words to close the sale. Try to anticipate your prospect's questions and objections and have the answers and counters ready. You can't win a war by firing your closing salvo from back at the bivouac.

3. **Thief #3—Erratic scheduling:** To get the most out of your day, learn to run an internal time clock. Be on the job at eight o'clock sharp and stay on the job until five or six o'clock. To be truly productive, successful professionals

work a minimum 45-hour week, and most find that productivity peaks at 50 hours. More than that tends to
result in burnout.

If you break your schedule on one day, you may find
it easier to break it again in the future. Waiting until 9
today will make it easier to postpone work until 10
tomorrow. Be tough with yourself. You chose to be a
salesperson because you wanted more out of life than
limited pay for limited hours.

4. **Thief #4—Waiting:** One of a salesperson's most baffling
problems is being on time for an appointment only to
end up waiting to see the customer. To avoid this, find
out ahead of time which hours your customer finds most
convenient and schedule your call between them. You
will save time and your customer will appreciate your
willingness to adjust to his or her schedule.

Second, don't turn the wait into an endurance con-
test. Give your customer 15 minutes as a courtesy, but
no more. Leave a message with the secretary that you
understand that he or she is busy, and you will call later
to arrange a better time for an appointment. Third, if the
call is important and you must wait, use this time to get
caught up on professional reading, paperwork, or
answering phone messages.

5. **Thief #5—Excessive talk:** When you go on sales calls,
you encounter all types of personalities. Some like to
shake hands and get right down to business; others like
to chitchat first and then ease into business talk; others
will combine a bit of both.

Although you may want to stop the chitchatty customer in mid-sentence, that may not be the best course. Let your customer talk for a little while, but try not to get too involved in the conversation. Keep your attention on your presentation and the reason you are there—to make a sale. At a tactful moment, steer the conversation back into your presentation.

6. **Thief #6—Lunch alone:** When a busy salesperson lunches alone, he or she is likely to order carelessly and eat too fast. Don't do it. A lump of fast food in your stomach can spoil your whole afternoon. Hunger is healthy; indigestion is not.

   Lunch with a customer gives you a pleasant setting away from the beehive of the customer's office. It's also one of the best ways to turn a prospect into a customer or to keep an existing customer satisfied. Besides, more business has been cemented over salad than stuffed between interrupting phone calls at the office.

7. **Thief #7—Paperwork:** If you use your cluttered desk as an excuse not to make sales calls, then this thief of time is lurking around every corner. If you have to start your day an hour to a half hour earlier to take care of paperwork, do it! Don't use valuable selling hours to fill out forms or enter computer data.

Never let any excuse keep you from selling for at least eight hours a day. Never start your professional reading until you have updated your daily records. Start today with a more organized approach to your precious selling hours. These are the jewels that can crown you king or queen.

CHAPTER 23

Self-Motivation Strategies

STAYING POSITIVE NO MATTER WHAT IS HAPPENING WITH YOUR SALES

Anybody can have a bad day. It might start out when you get to the office and find a note on your desk saying a long-time customer canceled an order. Then shipping calls and says they are running three days behind on deliveries. You are a half hour late for an appointment because you get stuck in traffic. The prospect you thought was in the bag is stalling and another is beating you up on terms. After only five minutes at the office, you may be asking yourself, "Why am I doing this?"

While the rewards of a sales career can be great, the profession is not for the fainthearted. It takes a resilient ego to handle all the rejection and problems that make up a salesperson's day and still stay pumped up.

"I tell my staff that today's a new day and yesterday died last night," says Jeffrey Roub, territory sales manager for the California State Automobile Association. "After all, Babe Ruth hit a lot of home runs, but he also struck out. You've got to swing the bat."

Roub is a firm believer in salespeople using motivational material to keep them in the right frame of mind. To that end, he sends out an e-mail newsletter every day to his 12 salespeople. "Topics range from working smarter to attitude and motivation, closing and follow-through techniques, and sales tips of the day," says Roub. "I concentrate on sales fundamentals because, in many cases, I feel salespeople don't revisit sales basics as often as they should."

Roub encourages salespeople to talk to their managers when they're feeling down or when things just don't seem to be going their way. "My job is to do everything I can do to help my people reach their goals, and I encourage my people to tell me how I can help," says Roub. "It may be a matter of actually going step-by-step through a difficult sales scenario, identifying what went wrong and how we can improve the next time through. It could be the salesperson needs more training, sales and motivational materials, or even additional sales leads. We try to continually reenergize our salespeople."

Ellen Burach, sales consultant for US Home Corporation, draws on the positive feedback she receives from satisfied customers to keep her up to speed. "Basically, I stay motivated by the positive feedback I receive from the people I work with, because I'm involved with my customers," says Burach. "It's the thank-you cards. I need that positive feedback and my buyers give it to me.

"Sure, I do get beat up and sometimes that's hard to accept," says Burach. "But the other side of that is when I see them smiling after a closing and they know they made the right decision and I helped them. I feel so good.

"I think about all the people I've helped and the positive things I've accomplished," says Burach. "Sometimes I feel like I sell water in the desert . . . I'm really doing a service. And the more I give, the more I receive."

Burach also feels that reading sales and motivational material helps when you're in a down mood. "I'm an avid reader of motivational books and I write down quotes in a journal that I read every morning," says Burach. "I also carry an obituary of someone I knew personally in my wallet. When I'm having a bad day, I take it out and read it and I don't feel so bad anymore. Every new day is a gift."

"It's OK to have problems because if I had no problems, I'd have no customers," says Burach.

FULL SELF-ESTEEM AHEAD: 10 WAYS TO CONVINCE YOURSELF THAT YOU ARE YOUR OWN BEST ASSET

Without confidence in yourself and your ability, it's unreasonable to expect your prospects and customers to have confidence in you. Many of us go through the occasional self-pitying, "I can't do anything right" phase, but the frequent rejections that salespeople experience require constant vigilance against bouts of low self-confidence. Use the following 10 tips to keep your self-esteem high and help you cultivate the can-do attitude that can boost motivation and sales.

1. **Study:** The more you know about your product and service, the more confidence you'll have presenting it and answering customer questions and objections. Knowing that your customers rely on you as a dependable source of information helps improve your perception of your value and worth as a competent professional. Broaden your horizons and strengthen your ties to your customers by reading up on their special hobbies or interests. Simply putting in the effort to improve yourself often helps boost self-esteem.

2. **Exercise:** Exercise has a great way of increasing your self-esteem along with your energy level and overall good health. If you're not pleased with your appearance, your negative self-image may be affecting your motivation. Adopt a consistent exercise program doing an activity you enjoy. Make time to walk for 30 minutes several times a week. Stick to your routine and chances are you'll eventually end up looking better and feeling better physically and emotionally.

3. **Listen:** If you can't seem to convince yourself of your limitless potential, let the motivational gurus do it for you. Take advantage of the endless supply of self-improvement and motivational tapes available. As you improve your self-esteem, concentrate on improving your listening skills as well. You may benefit with a better self-image and better sales.

4. **Finish:** Without a sense of accomplishment, it's more difficult to see yourself as a productive and contributing member of your sales team. Set deadlines that encourage

you to finish projects promptly. Complete call reports at the end of each day, and set a reasonable time limit within which to send follow-up letters or make follow-up calls. Make a daily to-do list and check off each task as you complete it. The more tasks you finish, the less work you'll have to weigh down your spirits.

5. **Encourage:** Selling is an emotionally demanding profession, so do your part to encourage and support the other salespeople in your office. Sometimes all it takes to raise your own spirits is a little effort to raise others'. Also, if you're always willing to motivate your team members, they'll likely return the favor when you're feeling less than gung ho.

6. **Search:** Examine your feelings to uncover the cause of your low self-esteem. Then look for solutions to the problems you find. Use the resources available to you to overcome barriers to your self-confidence. Ask other salespeople for advice or for some good person-to-person counseling. Instead of becoming a victim of your feelings, conduct an active search for ways to turn your attitude around.

7. **Talk:** Public speaking is often an excellent way to boost self-esteem. For many, speaking smoothly and powerfully to a captive audience is empowering and uplifting. Whether you make sales presentations to groups or one-on-one, public speaking can help you develop the poise and self-confidence that give your words greater selling impact. When your sales start to increase, your self-esteem should too.

8. **Endure:** With more peaks and valleys than the average roller coaster, selling's everyday stresses and disappointments can be damaging to one's self-esteem. Remind yourself that your prospects' rejection isn't personal, and that you have to listen to a certain number of no's before you can expect to hear a yes. When pessimism gets the better of you, remember the most difficult sale you ever made, and how determined you were to get it. Only through perseverance can you expect to make progress, so take the lows with the highs—your next sale might be just around the bend.

9. **Embrace:** Embrace selling as a profession. Make a mental list of all the reasons why you love your job. If you feel that you've got one of the best jobs in the world, daily setbacks may seem a little less important. Enjoy the little pleasures that your work brings you—a compliment from a customer, a pat on the back from a colleague or manager, and satisfaction that comes from giving 100 percent effort.

10. **Mentor:** Lend your guidance and support to another salesperson. The more you offer your time and assistance to others, the better you may feel about yourself. Acting as a mentor also places you in a position of importance—as a teacher and coach of another salesperson. With a sense of responsibility for another person's development, you're likely to feel more valued, and the respect and trust your "student" places in you helps you build and maintain your own self-esteem.

Everyone likes to feel important, valued, and worthy of others' respect. But in selling, when so much of one's performance hinges on motivation, a positive self-image is critical. Give yourself time to learn and overcome the problems and setbacks that can sabotage self-esteem. Remind yourself daily that success doesn't happen overnight but that you've got what it takes to make it happen eventually. Chances are, if you think you're a winner, you will be.

MOTIVATIONAL TIPS FOR GO-GETTERS

Priscella Peterson, a motivational speaker and the president of Management Recruiters Inc. of Lansing, Michigan, offers these golden nuggets for sales success.

"Celebrate your victories and reward yourself. Not just for closing a sale—it could be for getting a decision. If the decision is a no, celebrate it because it takes you one step closer to a yes. Reward yourself for getting past the gatekeeper or setting an appointment with a prospect.

Rewards don't have to be large; they can be small but special. Have your hair done, get your shoes shined, buy a sleeve of golf balls, or treat yourself to a special lunch. It's the action of rewarding yourself that adds to your enthusiasm.

Always remember that the big customers are out there just waiting for you to call. If you believe that they're out there, you'll make those calls and you'll have fun doing them. It's like hunting for a needle in a haystack and it can be challenging, but if you do your job, you'll find them.

When you reach your goals, immediately reevaluate where you are and then set new, higher goals. So often when we hit our goals we pat ourselves on the back for a job well done; then we become complacent and then just stop selling.

Keep yourself motivated by plastering pictures of your goals around your house, on your desk, and in your car. You may be working for a new Lincoln or Cadillac, a house, a boat, or a vacation home. Whatever it is, continuously remind yourself that you're working for a reason and visualize it."

CHAPTER 24

Managing Stress

LOW-STRESS SALES: CONTROL YOUR STRESS BEFORE IT CONTROLS YOU

In moderate to small amounts, stress is natural, and even desirable. It's a key ingredient in high productivity. Too much stress, however, poses a threat to physical and emotional well-being. For salespeople, job-related stress can easily escalate out of control.

When high stress becomes a way of life, vacations and time off are only quick fixes. You can't control fate, but you can take these seven steps to help ward off life-threatening stress for good. Stress and satisfaction often come from the same sources (work, family), so use these tips to ensure that stress doesn't keep you from enjoying the best things in life.

1. **Get tough:** You can cope effectively with setbacks and problems without dwelling on them. Do your best to solve problems, then clear any remaining negative

emotions from your mind. If you've done your best, the problem is out of your hands, so stop worrying about it. Negative feelings are draining and unproductive, and frazzled nerves often have undesirable physiological effects as well. Maintain inner peace by resisting and banishing bad feelings and anxiety-producing thoughts.

If you need help getting your thoughts and emotions under control, the market is flooded with self-help books, tapes, and videos.

2. **Limit responsibility:** Taking on too many obligations makes you less effective and productive all around. When you're too stressed to get any satisfaction from the commitments you make, you're probably making too many. Take on only obligations that you can comfortably handle. Spreading yourself too thin often means you get less accomplished, not more. Make a list of your priorities and spend your time accordingly. Take responsibility for your own job, family, thoughts, and behaviors, and let others do the same.

3. **Learn and use effectiveness skills:** Know how to prioritize, delegate responsibility, and say no. These skills maximize work efficiency and represent the reduced-stress route to getting a job done. Avoid perfectionism and procrastination to work smarter. Constantly needing to catch up on work adds to stress, so streamline work habits and use schedules and priority lists to keep you in control at the office.

4. **Take physical and mental breaks:** To reduce stress, you must engage in activities that counter it. Take up a hobby

or an exercise regimen and stick with it. Know how to relax, play, and stop long enough to smell the roses. Taking a break sharpens your mind emotionally and intellectually, which increases productivity and decreases tension. Explore the concept of actually leaving town to take a break (that's right, vacation!).

5. **Prioritize activities:** Separate urgent and important tasks from less urgent, unimportant ones. Don't "chase rabbits" by dropping a high-priority task to pursue an urgent, low-priority one. When you concentrate your energy on high-stress projects, each step you take toward completing them should ease the stress they cause. You can't give everything 100 percent of your energy, so pick out the important things and distribute your time and attention among them.

6. **Take one day (project, disaster) at a time:** If you ever tried to stuff your mouth with corn, peas, steal, and mashed potatoes all at once, you'd probably find it difficult to focus on any one food. How, then, can anyone expect to effectively work on four or five projects at once? Quality work requires concentration and focus, which are difficult to attain when you're distracted by other demands. Reduce stress by temporarily working on one thing and putting aside everything else. Instead of juggling projects or commitments, use them to break your day or week into compartments. Living life and completing work in segments helps prevent you from feeling overwhelmed by either.

7. **Develop your spirituality:** Many people find peace and reduce stress through an active spiritual life. Whatever

your spiritual interest, try using it to channel or divert stress. Many people find their beliefs very uplifting and liberating, so explore your own spirituality as a means of reducing stress.

Stress often has a way of sneaking up on its victims. Because of their profession, salespeople are especially subject to high stress. Take stock of your life and weigh the satisfaction it brings you against the stress you normally feel. If the stress consistently outweighs the happiness, take control of your life, make some changes in your lifestyle and work habits, and rediscover your selling potential.

11 STEPS TO STRESS MANAGEMENT

Stress is an inescapable part of modern life. But you can change the way you react to it. The following suggestions for stress reduction will help you relax and enjoy life. As a dividend, you'll be more productive, so you'll create less stress for yourself in the future.

1. **Laugh:** Laughter is one of best tension releases there is. Find things to laugh about and people to laugh with. Laughter is a great antidote for taking life too seriously.

2. **Take breaks:** Learning to interrupt a stress-producing activity will help give you the break from tension that you need. You'll return to your activity refreshed and ready to be more productive.

3. **Make happy plans:** Anticipation is an exciting feeling. Plan to see a special movie, eat out with someone you like, or do something else that please you.

4. **Focus your thoughts:** The habit of thinking about too many things at the same time is extremely fatiguing and stress producing. Instead of being overwhelmed and unproductive, concentrate on one task at a time. Try making a list of other things you must do and then put it aside, so that you don't have to think about them— but you won't worry about forgetting them, either.

5. **Check yourself:** Stop to see if you are relaxed. Are your hands clenched? Is your jaw tight? Such tension will begin to spread throughout you body, so catch it early. Let your arms hang loosely, unwrinkle your brow, relax your mouth, and breathe deeply.

6. **Tackle the hardest jobs first:** This will give you a sense of tremendous accomplishment and provide momentum for finishing your other tasks. The pleasant things you must do will make your final hours at work enjoyable, if saved until last.

7. **Go task by task:** If you finish one task at a time, you will avoid feeling fragmented and overburdened. It is also easier to see where you're going with a job when you give it your full concentration. Leave some time between activities to minimize overlapping.

8. **Move:** Speed up you body action by moving to music, stretching, or taking a jog. Movement helps eliminate pent-up stress by aiding the removal of chemicals that stress produces and which make you feel bad.

9. **Manage your time:** Use a plan of action. Schedule only as many tasks each day as you can reasonably finish without pressure. Leave time in your schedule for the unexpected.

10. **Help someone and smile:** Lending a helping hand or smiling can do what other methods of relaxation can't do—they give you a wonderful feeling of happiness and well-being.

11. **Enjoy yourself now:** Stop whatever you're doing and delight in being alive. Sense the physical processes inside you, the good in people around you, and the beauty of the world you live in.

STRESS-REDUCING EXERCISES FOR THE BUSY SALESPERSON

You don't have to go to a gym to relax and feel refreshed.

Even simple stretching movements done at your desk, while waiting for an appointment, or behind the wheel of your parked car can help you uncoil tense muscles. Here are some quick samples from Barby Fairbanks Eide, owner of Professional Productions, who specializes in seminars for professionals and is certified in stress management by the Menninger Foundation.

1. **Deep breathing:** Close your eyes, take a deep breath, hold it for a count of 10, and let it out slowly. Repeat this five times.

2. **Visualization:** Close your eyes and picture that vacation you've been dreaming about (palm trees and sunbathing in a tropical resort or skiing down a frosty mountain top will do). Close your mind to other thoughts for a minute or two.

3. **Head relaxer:** Rotate your head to the right very slowly as far as it can go without straining. Then turn and rotate your head to the left the same way. Lean your head backward slowly, lifting your face up, and then forward to your chest.

4. **Pectoral stretch:** Grasp your hands behind your head. Press elbows as far back as you can. Hold for 10 seconds. Repeat.

5. **Side stretch:** Interlace your fingers and lift your arms overhead. Keep your elbows straight. Press your arms back as far as you can. Slowly lean to the left, then to the right.

6. **Shoulder relaxer:** Sitting or standing, raise your right shoulder and then drop it quickly. Repeat with the left shoulder. Raise both shoulders and rotate them backward three times, then repeat exercise rotating both shoulders forward.

7. **Foot relaxer:** Take off your shoes and wiggle your toes. If there is carpeting on the floor, work your toes, then the bottoms and sides of your feet into the carpet. Massage each toe, using gentle finger pressure over each joint. Also massage around your heel and around the top of your foot.

8. **Leg relaxer:** While sitting, lift your right leg with both hands from under the thigh and allow your calf and

ankle to swing freely from the knee. Repeat the exercise with the left leg.

9. **Arm and hand relaxer:** Stand up. Extend your arms in front of you at chest level and hold for count of 10. Lift arms above your head and clasp your hands. Stretch to the left side, then to the right, 10 counts each. Stretch and flex your muscles as much as possible. Drop your arms. Shake your right hand vigorously a few seconds, and repeat with the left hand.

10. **Eye relaxer:** Take visual breaks throughout the day. Relax eyes by changing focus. Look up from your work periodically and gaze out the window or down a hall. Consciously blink and take deep breaths. If your reading or paperwork is very intense, change focus frequently.

THE PRESSURE'S OFF: STRATEGIES FOR KEEPING YOUR SANITY AND RAISING YOUR SALES

For keeping you focused and motivated, moderate levels of stress are just what the doctor ordered. But when stress gets out of hand, you can take steps to bring it back down to a more productive level. Stick to these seven guidelines for thinking, working, and living to ensure that your stress works for you instead of against you.

1. **Look on the bright side:** Stress is largely a matter of perception. By looking for the good in a seemingly bad situation, you can change for the better the way you perceive your circumstances. When a stressor appears, ask yourself, "Is there a better way of interpreting this situation? Will

this matter three years from now?" For example, if you are terrified by the idea of giving a presentation to 100 prospects, think of what a great opportunity it is. When you suffer disappointments, remember that setbacks always offer growth lessons and failure is key to success.

2. **Keep on growing:** By resisting change, you actually give up security; while the rest of the world grows and improves, you stay in the same rut. Accept that change is inevitable and resolve to embrace it. Make a habit of self-improvement by reading for 30 minutes a day, attending regular training seminars, and listening to educational and motivational tapes in your car. By expanding your knowledge base, you will not only thrive on changes to come but also add value to your organization.

3. **Get your priorities straight:** As Confucius once noted, "The man who chases two rabbits catches neither," so think about the activities that make the best use of your time and devote yourself only to them. Set short-, medium-, and long-term goals for yourself and outline a series of steps to help you reach them. Then list the activities required to reach each step and make those activities your priority.

4. **Plan your time wisely:** If you don't schedule your priorities in your daily planner, someone else's priorities will end up filling it, and the tasks you didn't get done may boost stress levels. Every Sunday night, set aside 30 minutes for a weekly planning session. Ask yourself, "What goals do I need to accomplish over the next seven days for me to feel this week was a success?" Make a note of these goals, then make room for them in your daily organizer. Divide your

days into blocks devoted to different activities so you waste less time making transitions between them.

5. **Manage your environment:** None of us lives in a bubble, which means all the information, circumstances, and people we expose ourselves to must affect us. Be aware of how these factors affect you—if watching the news leaves you anxious or depressed, your time might be better spent blowing off steam on a vigorous walk. Assess your environment carefully to identify stressors that might have gone unnoticed. Associate with positive people and surround yourself with uplifting messages in your office and your car. Gandhi once said, "I will not let anyone walk through my mind with their dirty feet," and neither should you.

6. **Stop and smell the roses:** Taking time for yourself is critical. Schedule time in your planner each week to commune with nature, listen to relaxing music, or get a massage—anything that helps you unwind and regain perspective. Put the power of visualization and meditation to work for you to help you stay calm and collected. By taking a few moments each week to rejuvenate yourself, you will make the rest of the week more productive.

Many people are vulnerable to stress simply because they don't recognize it or know how to fight it. Although we can't drop everything and jet off to the Caribbean every time a crisis arises, we can learn to combat stress and diminish its effects. Take your own stand against stress and you will likely find yourself enjoying selling more and enjoying more sales.

CHAPTER 25

Success Principles

BETTER SALES PERFORMANCE IN EIGHT STEPS

To stay ahead of the competition, great salespeople, like great athletes, must perform at a slightly higher level than those around them. For a foolproof way to maximize your potential, act on recognized performance psychologist J. Mitchell Perry's eight principles for taking your sales performance to new heights.

Four Steps to Surging

1. **Ritualize—Develop a gladiator mentality:** To sharpen your focus and create momentum, start with a ritual. NFL wide receiver Jerry Rice is precise about pregame preparation, which Rice's coach Bill Walsh calls the gladiator mentality. Think about how you need to prepare

to do your best on a sales call, then do it before every appointment.

2. **Visualize—See a mental movie:** Before he hits every shot, golf legend Jack Nicklaus previews it in his mind. Get yourself in a winning frame of mind by envisioning your success before you actually attempt to achieve it. Picture yourself giving a smooth, compelling presentation, the impressed expressions on your prospects' faces, and how you'll feel leaving with a signed order.

3. **Optimize—Turn it up and just do it:** When the time comes, put your fear aside and go for it. Learn to trust in your own ability enough that fear of failure doesn't overpower you. Prepare thoroughly so you don't have a legitimate reason to be afraid, then just take the plunge.

4. **Capitalize—Celebrate your success:** When you celebrate your success, you give yourself credit for being able to achieve great things, which builds your confidence and helps you to repeat your performance. Microsoft founder Bill Gates says that what he does best is share his enthusiasm: Learn to share yours by giving yourself a pat on the back when you deserve one.

Four Steps to Recovering from Setbacks

1. **Check your self-awareness level:** The way you react to setbacks largely determines how quickly and effectively you'll recover from them. The next time things don't go your way, ask yourself if you're overreacting to the

situation and how you can react mentally and physically in more constructive ways.

2. **Weigh all your options:** Instead of seeing things in black or white—only in terms of success or failure—give yourself more options. Consider all the ways in which you might handle a problem, then choose the one that's most likely to work best for you. NBA great Michael Jordan creates new success options when he reminds himself that "there will always be another chance in another game."

3. **Draw conclusions:** When you make a mistake, analyze it and identify what you need to do to avoid repeating it. Remember the cause-and-effect relationship between what you do and what you get. Use your mistakes as learning experiences to make you a smarter and more effective salesperson.

4. **Make changes:** Remember that improvement comes only through change. Once you identify the causes of your past mistakes or current lackluster performance, design a plan with action steps for improvement. Don't be afraid to consider new and unusual ways of looking for and approaching prospects and closing sales.

Get SMART: Five Goal-Setting Tips to Make Your Aims More Achievable

Goals are a great way to motivate yourself and boost productivity, but if you fail to meet them, they can have the opposite effect. To make sure your goals improve your odds of success, make them SMART: Specific, Measurable, Attainable, Realistic, and Tangible. By following these rules for better goal setting, you'll boost your motivation for selling and enjoy the rewards that result:

1. **Specific:** It's not enough to say that you want to make more money or own an expensive sports car—your goals have to be even more specific. How much more money do you want to earn? Exactly what kind of sports car do you dream of owning? For every goal you set, make sure you know precisely what you want, what action steps will help you get it, and when you plan to reach it. Give some serious thought to what motivates you—travel? recognition? money?—and set your goals accordingly. Develop a mental image of yourself achieving your specific goal and keep it in mind to keep you motivated.

2. **Measurable:** Goals are effective motivators partly because they allow you to measure how far you've come and how far you have to go. When your goal is specific, it's easier to measure. To make your goal measurable, ask yourself exactly what you need to accomplish to reach it. If you want a new big-screen TV, for example, you might need to earn an extra $5,000 in commissions. You can make your goal measurable by breaking down the total amount of money you need into the amount of extra money you'll need each month. For less tangible goals, break the goal down into monthly percent increases in sales or productivity. Mark your calendar with the dates when you'll check your goals, than be sure to stay on schedule so you can meet them on time.

3. **Attainable:** It's great to aim high, but remember that Rome wasn't built in a day. When your goals are too lofty, your chances of reaching them are worse, and falling short can be demotivating. Compare your goals to your past performance. The idea is to challenge yourself to improve your performance—not attempt the impossible. Compare your sales figures from several months and quarters past, and use them to compute an average monthly or quarterly increase. Let that average serve as a guide for setting a reasonable goal.

4. **Realistic:** Your goals must be realistic. If you're new to sales and competing against seasoned sales veterans, making it your goal to be the company's top salesperson within three months probably isn't realistic. Make sure your goals don't let you down by knowing your strengths and weaknesses before you set them. Consider the forces beyond your control that may affect your ability to reach them. You don't want to impose limits on yourself, but unrealistic goals can be just as counterproductive. Think about such resources as training, time, motivational support, or self-discipline and whether you'll have them in sufficient measure to succeed. If not, set your sights a little low for the time being, or find out how you can get what you need.

5. **Tangible:** Your goal will have longer-lasting impact if you have a tangible symbol to remind you of reaching it. Recognition from a CEO or manager, for instance, may take the form of a plaque or personal note you can keep as a future motivator. As a tangible symbol of meeting a

goal of higher commissions or a pay raise, hold on to your paycheck stub or use the money to buy something to stand as a symbol of your success. With a reward for meeting your goals that you can see, you'll help motivate yourself to consistently higher levels of sales success.

Ongoing improvement is a cornerstone of long-term sales success. For consistent improvement, you need goals that hold you to ever-higher standards of performance. With carefully planned goals, you can help ensure that each passing year makes you a smarter, stronger, and more efficient salesperson.

CREDITS

"Prospecting: Developing New Leads" was written by Renee Houston Zemanski and previously published in *Selling Power.*

"Tips for Generating Leads" was written by Steve Atlas and previously published in *Selling Power.*

"Tips for Generating Gold Sales Nuggets From Your Prospecting Efforts" was written by Malcolm Fleschner and previously published in *Selling Power*.

"10 Ways to Generate Leads through Networking" was written by Christine Neuberger and was previously published in *Selling Power* as "Networking Works."

"Once You Have a Lead, Give Them the VIP Treatment" was written by Nicki Joy and was previously published in *Selling Power* as "Give Your Buyer a Boost: Pumped-Up Prospects Can Help Inflate Your Sales."

"How to Handle Cold Calls with Ease" was written by Andrea J. Moses and previously published in *Selling Power*.

"Steps to Cold Calls that Close Every Time" was written by Paul Andrew and previously was published in *Selling Power* as "Six-Step Cold Calls."

"14 Field-Tested Tips for Cold-Calling on the Phone" was written by Rebecca L. Morgan and was previously published in *Selling Power* as "Fourteen Cold-Calling Telephone Tips to Warm Your Sales Pitch."

"Appointment-Setting Tips" was written by John Fellows and previously published in *Selling Power*.

"Tips to Improve Your B2B Teleselling Efforts" was written by Malcolm Fleschner and previously published in *Selling Power*.

"Getting Past Voice Mail: How to Utilize Voice Mail to Your Advantage" was written by William F. Kendy and previously published in *Selling Power*.

"Maximize Your Voice Mail Message" was written by Malcolm Fleschner and previously published in *Selling Power*.

"To Add Urgency, Have an Angle" was written by Malcolm Fleschner and previously published in *Selling Power*.

"Getting Customers to Call Back" was written by Dave Brock and previously published in *Selling Power*.

"Write Sales Letters That Work" was written by Ed Werz and previously published in *Selling Power*.

"Energize Your Sales Letters" was written by Ray Dreyfack and previously published in *Selling Power*.

"Harness the Power of the Written Word" was written by William F. Kendy and previously published in *Selling Power*.

"Clear E-mails Are the Key to Success" was written by Kim Wright Wiley and previously published in *Selling Power*.

"Tips for Effective E-mail" was written by Malcolm Fleschner and previously published in *Selling Power*.

"Using E-mail to Your Advantage" was written by Malcolm Fleschner and was previously published in *Selling Power* as "Get the E-mail Advantage."

"Tips for Using E-mail to E-Sell" was written by Malcolm Fleschner and previously published in *Selling Power*.

"When to Use E-mail—and When Not To" was written by Malcolm Fleschner and previously published in *Selling Power*.

"Skill Set" was written by Steve Atlas and previously published in *Selling Power*.

"Writing Better Proposals" was written by Vince Reardon and previously published in *Selling Power*.

"Writing Proposals Your Customers Can't Refuse" was written by John Fellows and was previously published in *Selling Power* as "A Decent Proposal: Here's How to Write Proposals Your Customers Just Can't Refuse."

"Put the 'Pro' in Proposal" was written by Malcolm Fleschner and previously published in *Selling Power*.

"Strategies for Every Stage of the Proposal Process" was written by Renee Houston Zemanski and was previously published in *Selling Power* as "How to Write Winning Proposals."

"Packing Persuasion in Your Writing" was written by Renee Houston Zemanski and was previously published in *Selling Power* as "The Power of Persuasive Writing."

"Essential Strategies for Boosting Trade Show Leads" was written by Heather Baldwin and previously published in *Selling Power*.

"Quick Trade Show Tips" was written by Carolee Boyles and previously published in *Selling Power*.

"How to Turn Your Next Trade Show Appearance into a Promotional Extravaganza" was written by Malcolm Fleschner and was previously published in *Selling Power* as "No Business Like Trade Show Business."

"Getting the Most from Every Trade Show" was written by Mark S. A. Smith and was previously published in *Selling Power* as "Greatest Trade Show on Earth."

"Profit-Boosting Ideas to Help Trade-Show-Shy Salespeople" was written by Mim Goldberg and previously published in *Selling Power*.

"Tips from a Trade Show Trainer" was written by Steve Atlas and previously published in *Selling Power*.

"Increase Your Sales with Customer Satisfaction Surveys" was written by Barry J. Farber and previously published in *Selling Power*.

"Tips for Finding Out Just What Your Customers Are Thinking" was written by Malcolm Fleschner and previously published in *Selling Power*.

"A Position of Authority: How to Develop New Leads into Qualified Prospects Who Have the Authority to Buy" was written by Steve Atlas and previously published in *Selling Power*.

"Seven Tips for Qualifying" was written by William F. Kendy and previously published in *Selling Power*.

"Using Relationship Building to Get More out of Your Best Accounts" was written by Carolee Boyles and previously published in *Selling Power*.

"Tips to Building Rapport with Your Customers" was written by Malcolm Fleschner and was previously published in *Selling Power* as "Rich Man, Rapport Man".

"Creative Ways to Stand Out from the Crowd" was written by Pam Lonton and was previously published in *Selling Power* as "How to Stand Out from the Crowd."

"Be Invisible to Customers" was written by Daryl Allen and previously published in *Selling Power*.

"Always Focus on Service" was written by Heather Baldwin and was previously published in *Selling Power* as "May I Serve You?"

"How to Repair Troubled Customer Relationships" was written by Malcolm Fleschner and previously published in *Selling Power*.

"Your Ally, the Gatekeeper" was written by Renee Houston Zemanski and previously published in *Selling Power*.

"Get Your Foot in the Door: 10 Appointment-Setting Techniques that Keep You in Front of Customers" was written by John Fellows and previously published in *Selling Power*.

"Appointment-Setting Tips" was written by John Fellows and previously published in *Selling Power*.

"Creative Ways for Tackling any Block" was written by Malcolm Fleschner and previously published in *Selling Power*.

"The Challenge of Your Competition" was written by Chuck Reaves and previously published in *Selling Power*.

"Tips for Luring Customers Away from the Competition" was written by Malcolm Fleschner and previously published in *Selling Power*.

"Head Off the Competition" was written by Malcolm Fleschner and previously published in *Selling Power*.

"Competition Can Be Your Winning Game" was written by Carl K. Clayton and previously published in *Selling Power*.

"What Does Your Customer Want? was written by Malcolm Fleschner and was previously published in *Selling Powe* as "'But' Out Selling: Get Past Tense to Make Your Future Perfect."

"Tips for Exposing the Customer Needs that Lead to Sales Opportunities" was written by Malcolm Fleschner and previously published in *Selling Power*.

"Think Like Your Customer" was written by Malcolm Fleschner and previously published in *Selling Power* as "Inquiring Minds."

"How to Elevate Your Value in Customers' Eyes" was written by Malcolm Fleschner and previously published in *Selling Power*.

"Sell Value before You Quote Price" was written by Jim Estrada and previously published in *Selling Power*.

"How to Add Value To Every Sales Call" was written by Graham Roberts-Phelps and previously published in *Selling Power*.

"Presentation Polish" was written by Sondra Brewer and previously published in *Selling Power*.

"Tips for Getting Pumped Up before Show Time" was written by Renee Houston Zemanski and was previously published in *Selling Power* as "Presentation Planner."

"Five Tips for Handling Q&A Session Like A Pro" was written by Renee Houston Zemanski and previously published in *Selling Power*.

"Please a Crowd: Tips for Effective Group Presentations" was written by Malcolm Fleschner and previously published in *Selling Power*.

"Beef Up Your Presentation Package: Five Tips for Leaving a Lasting Positive Impression" was written by Margaret Bedrosian and previously published in *Selling Power*.

"10 Tips for Voice Improvement" was written by Jeffrey Jacobi and previously published in *Selling Power*.

"Mirror, Mirror (and Other Persuasive Tips)" was written by *Selling Power* Editors and previously published in *Selling Power*.

"Tips for Selling across the Light Spectrum" was written by Malcolm Fleschner and previously published in *Selling Power*.

"Giving the Right Signals" was written by Christine Neuberger and previously published in *Selling Power*.

"How to Negotiate with Purchasing Managers" was written by Renee Houston Zemanski and previously published in *Selling Power*.

"Five Tips for Negotiating Like a Pro" was written by Malcolm Fleschner and previously published in *Selling Power*.

"Negotiating Tips for Your Sales Career" was written by Malcolm Fleschner and was previously published in *Selling Power* as "Make An Offer No One Can Refuse: Tips for Negotiating Your Best Deal after You've Sold Yourself."

"Negotiate for a Win-Win" was written by Christine Neuberger and was previously published in *Selling Power* as "Sucessful Negotiations."

"Negotiation Tips for Dealing with a Demanding Buyer" was written by Steve Atlas and previously published in *Selling Power*.

"Sell the Big Picture" was written by Joan Leotta and previously published in *Selling Power*.

"It's a Stall World: How to Get Your Customers to Make a Decision" was written by Malcolm Fleschner and previously published in *Selling Power*.

"Four Quick Tips for Handling Objections" was written by Lain Ehman and previously published in *Selling Power*.

"Handling the Dreaded Price Objection" was written by Malcolm Fleschner and was previously published in *Selling Power* as "The Priceman Cometh."

"Proven Strategies for Handling Rejection" was written by Malcolm Fleschner and was previously published in *Selling Power* as "Hit the 'Reject' Button."

"Objection Prevention" was written by Rick Phillips and previously published in *Selling Power*.

"To Close . . . Try the Porcupine Technique" was written by Don Farrant and previously published in *Selling Power*.

"Clinch the Close with Better Questions" was written by Ronald Karr and previously published in *Selling Power*.

"How to Close a Sale without Causing Prospect Panic" was written by Len D'innocenzo and previously published in *Selling Power*.

"Getting Past Yes" was written by Malcolm Fleschner and previously published in *Selling Power*.

"Upselling Requires Knowing the Customer's Needs and Being Prepared to Offer Options" was written by William F. Kendy and previously published in *Selling Power*.

"Win Sales with Follow-Up" was written by Christine Neuberger and previously published in *Selling Power*.

"The Ideal Follow-Up Plan" was written by Renee Houston Zemanski and previously published in *Selling Power*.

"Follow Up, Up, and Away" was written by Malcolm Fleschner and previously published in *Selling Power*.

"Five Aggressive Follow-up Strategies That Turn Hot Prospects into Big Profits" was written by W. Myers Barnes and was previously published in *Selling Power* as "Follow Up, Follow Through: Aggressive Follow-up Strategies Can Turn Hot Prospects into Big Profits."

"Effective Time Management" was written by Thomas P. Reilly and was previously published in *Selling Power* as "Three Tips for Effective Time Management."

"Smart Strategies for Managing Time Effectively" was written by Malcolm Fleschner and previously published in *Selling Power* as "Time Bandits."

"Seven Thieves of Time . . . That Can Steal Your Sales Away" was written by the *Selling Power* editors and previously published in *Selling Power*.

"Phone Time Management Skills" was written by Heather Baldwin and previously published in *Selling Power*.

"Staying Positive No Matter What Is Happening with Your Sales" was written by William F. Kendy and previously published in *Selling Power*.

"Full Self-Esteem Ahead: 10 Ways to Convince Yourself that You are Your Own Best Asset" was written by Daryl Allen and previously published in *Selling Power*.

"Low-Stress Sales: Control Your Stress before It Controls You" was written by Steve Simms and previously published in *Selling Power*.

"11 Steps to Stress Management" was written by Pat Garnett and previously published in *Selling Power*.

"Stress-Reducing Exercises for the Busy Salesperson" was written by Barby Fairbanks Eide and previously published in *Selling Power* as "Stress Reducers for the Busy Salesperson."

"The Pressure's Off: Strategies for Keeping Your Sanity and Raising Your Sales" was written by Robin Sharma and previously published in *Selling Power*.

"Better Sales Performance in Eight Steps" was written by Dr. J. Mitchell Perry and previously published in *Selling Power*.

"Get SMART: Five Goal-Setting Tips to Make Your Aims More Achievable" was written by David J. Lill and previously published in *Selling Power*.

"Reach for Success" was written by Mary-Ellen Drummond and previously published in *Selling Power*.

"Tips Are Tops" was written by Ray Dreyfack and previously published in *Selling Power*.

INDEX

ABOUT THE AUTHOR

A dual citizen of both Austria and the United States, Gerhard Gschwandtner is the founder and publisher of *Selling Power*, the leading magazine for sales professionals worldwide, with a circulation of 165,000 subscribers in 67 countries.

© Hisham Bharoocha

He began his career in his native Austria in the sales training and marketing departments of a large construction equipment company. In 1972 he moved to the United States to become the company's North American Sales Training Director, later moving into the position of Marketing Manager.

In 1977 he became an independent sales training consultant, in 1979 creating an audiovisual sales training course called the Languages of Selling. Marketed to sales managers at Fortune 500 companies, the course taught nonverbal communication in sales together with professional selling skills.

In 1981 Gerhard launched *Personal Selling Power*, a tabloid-format newsletter directed to sales managers. Over the years the tabloid grew in subscriptions, size, and frequency; the name changed to *Selling Power*; and in magazine format it became the leader in the professional sales field. Every year *Selling Power* publishes the Selling Power 500, a listing of the largest sales forces in America. The company publishes books, sales training posters, and audio and video products for the professional sales market.

Gerhard Gschwandtner has become America's leading expert on selling and sales management. He conducts Webinars for such companies as SAP, and *Selling Power* has recently launched a new conference division which sponsors and conducts by-invitation-only leadership conferences directed toward companies with high sales volume and large sales forces.

For more information on *Selling Power*, its products, and services, please visit www.sellingpower.com.

Subscribe to *Selling Power* today and close more sales tomorrow!

GET 10 ISSUES – INCLUDING THE SALES MANAGER'S SOURCE BOOK.

In every issue of *Selling Power* magazine you'll find:

■ **A Sales Manager's Training Guide** with a one-hour sales training workshop complete with exercises and step-by-step instructions. Get a new guide in every issue! Created by proven industry experts who get $10,000 or more for a keynote speech or a training session.

■ **Best-practices reports** that show you how to win in today's tough market. Valuable tips and techniques for opening more doors and closing more sales.

■ **How-to stories** that help you speed up your sales cycle with innovative technology solutions, so you'll stay on the leading edge and avoid the "bleeding edge."

■ **Tested motivation ideas** so you and your team can remain focused, stay enthusiastic and prevail in the face of adversity.

Plus, you can sign up for five online SellingPower.com newsletters absolutely FREE.